RADICAL LOVE
IN A BROKEN WORLD
RON NIKKEL

RADICAL
L❤VE
IN A BROKEN WORLD
RON NIKKEL

CHRISTIAN
FOCUS

Ron Nikkel is the President of Prison Fellowship International, a global association of national Prison Fellowship organizations in 117 countries whose mission is to mobilize and assist the Christian community in its ministry to prisoners, ex-prisoners, victims and their families. He travels extensively and has visited more than 1,000 prisons in 120 countries.

He is a Canadian and resides in Cape Breton Island, Nova Scotia, with his wife Celeste and their two Border collies.

Unless otherwise noted, all Scripture quotations are from the NIV (*Holy Bible New International Version*, Copyright © 1973, 1978, 1984 by the International Bible Society, Zondervan Bible Publishers);

Scripture quotations marked NEB are taken from the *New English Bible* © Oxford University Press and Cambridge University Press 1961, 1970

Scripture quotations marked NASB are taken from the *New American Standard Bible* ®, Copyright © 1960, 1962, 1963, 1968, 1971, 1972, 1973, 1975, 1977, 1995 by The Lockman Foundation Used by Permission. (www.lockman.org)

© Ron Nikkel
ISBN 978-1-84550-702-2

Published in 2011
by
Christian Focus Publications,
Geanies House, Fearn, Ross-shire,
IV20 1TW, Great Britain.
www.christianfocus.com

Printed by Nørhaven A/S, Denmark

Cover design by DUFI-art.com

Contents

A PREFACE

When the Christian consciously keeps faith with his Lord,
he is led to the least of these,
the brethren of the Lord,
and to the Lord Himself.

JACQUES ELLUL

PROLOGUE

FEAR clutched the pit of my stomach as the plane touched down on the bumpy runway and taxied to a stop in front of a dilapidated terminal building. I was among only a handful of people who disembarked and was rather apprehensive as we walked a short distance toward the sand-bagged terminal entrance. Heavily armed soldiers watched our every move.

For two days I had unsuccessfully attempted to contact a man with whom I had been corresponding for more than a year. I questioned my sanity for accepting his invitation to visit him as civil conflict was tearing his country apart. But I was naïve and curious, deeply touched by the man's evident courage and compassion in reaching out to prisoners, combatants, and common offenders, amid the bloodshed and unrelenting turmoil of the conflict.

I grew up amid the comfortable atmosphere of a middle-class family in a small town where being Christian and going to church was part of our culture. Yet for the most part my life reflected a bland and passionless faith that was characterized by believing the right things, being active in the church and avoiding bad habits.

In more recent years, I had taken a small risk of faith by becoming involved with Prison Fellowship International. I found myself increasingly captivated by the examples of men and women who, even amid extreme difficulty and danger, followed Jesus in the way of justice, mercy, and truth, regardless of personal cost and threat of opposition. That's why I am here, I remembered. The people I had come to see were risking their lives daily reaching out to petty criminals and terrorists, and helping their families in the name of Jesus.

After enduring questioning by a very demanding immigration official concerning the purpose of my visit and having my luggage searched for weapons, I made my way to the airport exit. The only people there were waiting for me. I was relieved! The warmth and enthusiasm with which they greeted me was such a contrast to the tension I felt. But the tension was not entirely gone as we drove down deserted roads, through multiple military checkpoints and past trucks crammed full of young men in battle gear. Again I wondered why anyone would risk his life to do good for prisoners in the middle of a civil war.

As we drove into the capital, my hosts talked about the men and women they were visiting in prison: violent people whose lives were being transformed from hostility and hatred to love and peace. They talked about the growing fellowship of prisoners who were turning their backs on crime and violence in spite of the fact that the prison was a dangerous place.

I spent a sleepless night hearing the unfamiliar sounds of explosion and gunfire, some of them real and undoubtedly some by-products of my hyper-tensed imagination. The next morning the drive to prison did nothing to lessen my anxiety. Along the broken roads and among crumbling buildings life seemed almost normal, yet signs of devastation and conflict were clearly evident. My heart pounded as we approached the looming stone walls of the prison, even though I knew, paradoxically, we would probably be safer inside than out.

A ragged group of prisoners was gathered in the central courtyard as we entered the prison. Some were rebels and others ordinary civilian criminals, most of them part of the Christian fellowship group. The light in their eyes was in stark contrast to their drab and dreary surroundings. I could see the hope and feel the joy among that group of men as several of them shared their stories of finding hope and life in Jesus Christ.

After meeting with the group, I was taken to meet prisoners who were being held in secure confinement. Passing row upon row of dark foul-smelling cells I unexpectedly came face to face with a young prisoner who was leaning against the bars of his solitary cell smoking the nub of a cigarette pressed tightly to his lips. The intensity in his eyes stopped me in my tracks.

He is far too young to be a terrorist! I exclaimed to myself. Flashing brown eyes and the sharp features of his face betrayed nothing of the violence and bloodshed of his involvement with a rebel group. The young prisoner steadily returned my gaze through the steel bars of his cell door. I found myself gripped by the heart-wrenching story of his life. An unrepentant rebel with a cause, he was determined to avenge the injustice of the government in power, seeing it as responsible for the desperate poverty of his people. His eyes blazed as he talked about the revolution and his hatred of the regime he held responsible for his family's suffering and his father's "disappearance."

When he finished telling us his story, his face hardened and he spat contemptuously on the floor. "Of what use am I in here?" he hissed. "That fat pig president, he should suffer in here and die like a starving rat. The revolution needs me in the streets, not in this rotten pit where nobody cares if I live or die."

"God cares," I responded, almost automatically.

The prisoner's knuckles whitened as he clenched the iron bars which separated us. "Why does God let rich, evil men torment and exploit our people?" he retorted. His fevered eyes smoldered with untold pain and through his gritted teeth he cried, "Why is your God always with the rich and powerful?"

Numbly I looked back at him, unable to respond as he glared at me. His question seemed to ricochet off the tomb-like prison walls. What answer could I give? Common, empty platitudes careened uselessly through my mind and the reeking prison air burned my eyes and throat. I had to break away from his gaze. I felt I had nothing meaningful to say to him, but I couldn't turn my back and walk away even though I desperately wanted to move on to another cell. As I stood there the realization came to me that I could possibly be the only messenger of God's love he might ever hear.

"Jesus knows exactly what you are experiencing," I continued. "He was once a prisoner betrayed by a person He trusted, falsely accused, arrested, completely abandoned, imprisoned, tortured, and a victim of total injustice." "But He did not fight back," I continued. "You know that violence only causes more hatred and more suffering. But Jesus did something more radical than any rebel. He forgave His enemies and overcame their hatred with love." He listened impassively as I spoke about Jesus. To him God had always seemed remote and Jesus was confined to the world of churches and old ladies. Although I knew my words were true, they felt so empty and meaningless in the darkness of the young man's anguish.

The idea that Jesus actually cares about people in their everyday suffering was completely foreign to him, and it is completely foreign to most people in or out of prison who suffer for whatever reason. To many people in our world Jesus is completely unknown or, at best, is only a remote and disconnected historical figure, spoken of in churches on Sunday, and possibly of spiritual help to some people but completely unrelated to their experience. It seems to them that God doesn't know and doesn't care and doesn't act. So all that a person can do is stand up and fight for himself, if he is able to do that.

I understood why it was so difficult for that young rebel prisoner to connect with what I was telling him. He was undeniably a victim of injustice and exploitation. His family was suffering in excruciating poverty and degradation, and he saw no other hope than to fight for the cause of the revolution, even if that meant death. After a few moments we left him and walked through the prison wing, stopping here and there to speak with other inmates. As I watched and listened to my friends interacting with the prisoners, I saw their actions in a new light. They were not only courageous in the midst of conflict, they were the true revolutionaries. While rebels were fighting against injustice, my friends were actually bringing hope to people in the midst of desperation. It dawned on me that in the godforsaken experiences of those prisoners, the only touch of God's grace they might ever experience is the understanding, love, and help of the men and women I was with.

Several hours later, as we emerged from the wretched prison, the young rebel's question still haunted me. "Of what use am I to the revolution in here?" It was as if the question was meant for me. "Of what use is my faith if I can't live it out? Of what use am I to the cause of Jesus if I stay imprisoned in the security of a spiritual cell?"

What Jesus did so many centuries ago among a captive suffering people is re-enacted again and again in the most unexpected places and in the least likely lives. My experience in that prison is one of many through which I have increasingly come to see that faith in Jesus is not a religion, ideology, church membership or even the recitation of a doctrinal creed. Faith in Jesus is literally a radical way of living our lives, of following Him into the dark, depressing, deadening places of human experience to love and care for those who are imprisoned, whether their imprisonment is addiction, homelessness, physical illness, mental anguish, or literally confinement. Having faith in Jesus should make a difference in the world!

I am still learning that the most revolutionary aspect of being a radical follower of Jesus has little to do with believing things that other people don't believe and everything to do with being courageous, taking risks, and getting personally involved with the needy, undeserving, and unbelieving. Within the very bowels of society an invisible revolution began taking root two thousand years ago amongst the politically disconnected, socially inconsequential, and the economically powerless. It was revolutionary in that God became fully human in the person of Jesus in order to love, forgive, heal, and help human beings in the real world, in real time.

What I experienced in the dank prison of a country torn apart by conflict was the beginning of a journey. I saw rebels whose lives were transformed, not by a revolutionary cause, but by the radical love of Jesus expressed through people who dared to care. For the first time in my life I began thinking seriously about how radical the way of Jesus Christ is in transforming human life. Jesus didn't only proclaim the light of God's truth; He is the light. And after teaching His followers He turned to them and said, "You are the light of the world" (Matt. 5:14).

To be a Christian is to follow in the way of Jesus, learning to think and speak and act like Him, not literally, but in the radical way of loving and caring for people as He did. This is a way beyond mere belief, a truly revolutionary way that makes all the difference in the world.

Dare to be a different kind of Christian. Dare to make a difference!

Part A

Beyond Belief: Being Good News in a Bad News World

———◆———

CHAPTER 1

CAN YOU SEE WHAT I'M SAYING?

"Can you see what I'm saying?" a young woman asked her friend, with excitement rising in her voice. "Do you see what I mean?" she asked breathlessly, without waiting for an answer.

What an odd thing to ask someone, I thought to myself, if she means that question literally. How is it possible for anyone to see the words that another person is speaking? Most of us have ears by which we hear spoken words and eyes by which we see written words, not the other way around.

Of course, I knew that what she was really asking her friend was, "Do you understand what I'm saying? Can you 'see' it with your mind and not just hear it in your ears?" I have no idea what their conversation was about, but I began thinking about the implications of the question in terms of the messages we speak and the messages we live, What is it that people really "see" when they hear me talk about my faith or my beliefs?

Can anyone really see what I'm saying about the sanctity of life, if I support the call to execute convicted killers?

Can anyone see what I'm saying about the Christian worldview, if I turn my back on the immigrants from other cultures that seem to be invading our cities and towns? Can anyone see what I'm saying about the virtues of compassion and mercy as I walk down the street casually avoiding the outstretched hands and bleary eyes of the homeless and the drug-addled? Can anyone see what I'm saying about God's love and grace when I ignore and dismiss a person whose personality and style rubs me the wrong way? Can anyone see what I'm saying about integrity and truth as I avoid responsibility and take advantage of another person's weakness or incompetence?

Can anyone see what we Christians mean about the unconditional love of God when we insulate ourselves from the poor, the homeless, the imprisoned, and the mentally challenged, and criticize those who are sexually promiscuous, the drug-addicted, the inattentive, the hyperactive, and those whose politics are opposite to ours? Can anyone see what we mean about our unity in Jesus Christ when we dismiss other denominations as being liberal or conservative or steeped in tradition? Can anyone see what we are saying about the good news of the gospel—"for God so loved the world" (John 3:16)—when we pray against our enemies and accept the killing of innocents in the name of our own security concerns? Can anyone see what we are saying about giving generously to the needy while we first satisfy our own interests and desires in times of difficulty? Can anyone see what we mean by generosity when we demand every cent our friend owes before we will help her once again?

What do people really see when we speak about our faith and our beliefs? So often the words we speak are undermined and contradicted by what we do. The message we would really like to share with others is not the message they hear or see, because our actions speak louder than our words.

It is not uncommon for prisoners to tell me that Christians are all hypocrites. Sometimes it is just something they say because that is the word in the prison culture. But often I hear something else as well, I hear the disappointment and hurt of men and women who have yearned for good news, yet have seen bad news in the lives of those with good news to share. It is not so different on the streets, in the schools, in places of business, or even in our own neighborhoods and families.

What will it take for people to see what any of us is trying to say about the good news of the gospel, the good news about Jesus?

Chapter 2

JESUS WAS A "DO-GOODER"...

"So you've got another do-gooder on the show!" exclaimed a cynical caller during the closing moments of the phone-in radio program on which I was a guest.

The caller's meaning was clear. I had been speaking about compassionate justice, doing justice with mercy—going beyond retribution as a way of achieving justice by engaging offenders in a process of telling the truth, taking responsibility, making restitution, and reconciling with their victims. Admittedly, this is a more difficult approach to justice than the common notion that justice is accomplished when offenders are simply arrested, judged, and punished.

"Well, on that note as we come to the end of our show this morning, what have you got to say to that?" asked the host of the program, deflecting the do-gooder barb at me.

"There is a simple choice to make," I replied. "Would you rather that someone does good or would you prefer that a person does bad?" And with that we went off the air.

How has the term "do-gooder" become a term with such a negative connotation in society? Even Webster's English dictionary defines a do-gooder as being "a person who seeks to correct social ills in an idealistic, but usually impractical or superficial way." [1]

If doing good isn't practical or sensible, does that necessarily make it wrong or bad? Even as truth is sometimes inconvenient, but still true; so good can likewise be uncomfortable but still be good and right. The practicality of truth is not what determines whether it is true or not, nor does the perceived sensibility or convenience of a good action determine whether it is good or not.

I certainly do not like being dismissed as a mere do-gooder. In fact, I found the caller's comment a bit insulting. Yet the fact of the matter is that there is no future for either individuals or society if the cycle of evil is not broken by those who seek and do what is good in response. For neither by abdicating into apathy, nor by pursuing utilitarian [2] self-interest nor even by focusing on national security concerns, will the problem of crime and evil in society ultimately be undone.

Jesus taught the necessity of forgiveness in the face of insult and injury, of loving our enemies in the face of threat and aggression, and of doing good to those of evil intent who abuse and misuse us. It seems to me that by following Jesus I am compelled to follow Him in doing good even

---

1 Webster's *New World Dictionary of American English* (Simon & Schuster, New York; 1988).

2 See "utilitarian" moral theory which holds that an action is right (good) in proportion to the happiness that is produced. Happiness is defined as the intended pleasure and absence of pain. For an action or decision to be good it must be made on the basis of achieving the greatest good for the greatest number. It is held that the consequence of an action or decision is what makes it right (good).

when it appears illogical, foolish and impractical. Certainly there are times when compassion for others seems soft-headed; mercy for offenders seems weak-minded and grace for the undeserving seems irrational; and generosity to the irresponsible seems unwise. Yet if doing good in spite of all arguments to the contrary is in keeping with the good that Jesus taught, and if that means being a "do-gooder," I am probably on the right track.

The world needs more "do-gooders," people who are totally passionate about following in the way of Jesus by seeking the welfare of the poor, pursuing peacemaking and alternatives to violence, and by being generous to a fault. The world needs men and women who joyfully and idealistically sacrifice themselves to share in and alleviate the suffering of the ill-begotten,

> the ill-informed,
>> the ill-fed,
>>> the ill-tempered,
>>>> the ill-motivated,
>>>>> the illegal,
>>>>>> and ill-treated people who live among us

In companionship with Jesus, who is "the word become flesh" (John 1:14), such people are the living embodiment of God's amazing grace, talking and walking the truth of God's love in a world that is fallen from grace.

> *"You are the light of the world. A city on a hill cannot be hidden.*
> *Neither do people light a lamp and put it under a bowl. Instead they put it on its stand, and it gives light to*

everyone in the house.

In the same way, let your light shine before men, that
they may see your good deeds and praise your
Father in heaven" (Matt. 5:14-16).

CHAPTER 3

LOOKING GOOD!

A beautiful Fuji apple, my favorite variety, had been on my desk all day and I had been anticipating its sweet succulent taste. When finally the moment came, I picked it up and took a huge bite ... of disappointment. That glowing red apple was rotten at the core, an inedible superficial beauty!

Tossing it aside with no small measure of annoyance, I remembered that enigmatic story in the Gospels when Jesus and His hungry disciples approached a beautiful fig tree only to find it completely fig-less. Beautiful but barren! Even though it was not yet the season for figs, there should have been at least some budding evidence of fruit to come but the tree was just a good-looking tree without substance. Jesus cursed that disappointing tree as He and the disciples continued their journey to the temple in Jerusalem. What He encountered upon entering the magnificent temple courts was even more of a disappointment than the fruitless fig tree. The sacred courtyards set aside for worship and prayer were humming with everyday commercial activity, a marketplace of buyers and sellers and currency exchangers (Mark 11:12-17).

Recently I was listening to a very challenging and stirring interview with a Rwandan clergyman on an American

Christian radio station who said, "It is about surrendering to the truth. These men know they don't deserve forgiveness; they don't deserve to live." The clergyman went on to tell the amazing story of killers in the genocide being totally transformed by the grace and mercy of God—forgiven. 'Now on their own free will they are doing something good with their hands, helping to build homes for their victims, the survivors of the massacre." [1]

"And now we'll take a short break with a message from our sponsors," interrupted the radio host. "We'll be right back after this. 'Dermitage! Look years younger with Dermitage! Guaranteed results fast! Free trial!'"

I could hardly believe my ears. I had just been listening to a man baring his soul and sharing the amazing truth of God's transforming power and reconciling love radically changing men from the inside out. And in the very next moment I found myself drawn into the seductive allure and importance of looking good, of recovering my youthful appearance. "What is going on here? How can they possibly do this? The seductive allure of looking good!" I muttered to myself. "What is the real message—the substance of the interview or the commercial? Just follow the money," I thought to myself. "There is no money in a painful story about forgiveness and reconciliation, but there is big money in pandering to people who long to look good."

The following morning I read a newspaper account about Thomas Pauli, a homeless ex-prisoner, a sex offender,

---

1 Bishop John Ruchyahana of Rwanda being interviewed on the Don Kroah radio show WAVA—January 16, 2009.

who had frozen to death on the streets of a city in America's Bible Belt the previous night because nobody would give him shelter for that bitter cold night.[2] A man froze to death in a rich city with an abundance of churches and Christian ministries, a city that prides itself on picturesque beauty and hospitality, and boasts that its "climate-controlled sky-walk and heated sidewalks will connect people to where they need to go!"[3]

It is tragic but true that we readily pay the price to keep ourselves looking good on the outside but shy away from the cost of producing the good fruit of compassion, forgiveness, and unconditional love. We often settle for appearances even as people around us hunger for the substance of the hope, love, and grace we espouse. To follow Jesus is not about keeping up appearances but about being "fruitful" in the good works of faith. And that is easier said than done! I think it is easier just to avoid the issue about the relative merits of believing the gospel to living it. On our own we are unable to do either!

> "You are the salt of the earth. But if the salt loses its saltiness, how can it be made salty again? ... You are the light of the world. A city on a hill cannot be hidden ... let your light shine before men, that they may see your good deeds and praise your Father in heaven" (Matt. 5:13-16).

---

2 *"Sex Offender Dies in Cold After Being Denied From Shelter"* (by Scott Michels, ABC News, January 30, 2009).

3 www.visitgrandrapids.org/visit.php

CHAPTER 4

BETWEEN THE MUSEUM
AND THE CHURCH

During the Soviet era I visited many churches in Russia, churches that had been preserved as museums, lifeless but filled with beautiful icons and artifacts of a once-vibrant and flourishing community of faith. The buildings and the accoutrements of religious observance had been preserved while the living church had not. On another occasion, while visiting Israel, a Palestinian Christian friend confided in me, "People come from all over the world to see the dead stones of holy places, the dead stones of Church history. Almost no one comes to Israel to be with us who are the 'living stones' of faith today. They are more interested in the lifeless stones of old churches than in the living church!"

Although museums are not usually places that I really enjoy visiting, I accepted an invitation to join the board of directors of our local museum. It is a modest museum for a small community and is dedicated to preserving the history and artifacts of our northern highlands and seafaring culture. In recent years the museum has played a leading role in promoting our old traditions of music and storytelling as a way of bringing the past into the present, a way of making history relevant and alive to people who know little about the rich heritage of our community.

Situated next to the museum is a hundred-year-old church that has been closed for a number of years. Recently the old church building was acquired by the museum and renovated into a community arts and culture center. Ironically, the museum sees little value in preserving the church as one of the oldest buildings in our area and the heart of community life in times gone by. Instead, it was converted into something that it never was. Yet such is the fate of many of the small churches that once dominated the cultural landscape of Cape Breton Island. Within just a few miles of my home, one church has been converted into an "esoteric wellness" center, another into a community hall; still another into a Gaelic Singers' hall, and now the church next to the museum is an arts and culture centre. Most of the remaining churches are also slowly dying out, destined to become the relics of a bygone era as fewer young people find anything attractive or relevant in the Church.

Unlike the beautifully preserved churches in Russia that had been converted into museums under Communist rule, the churches of Cape Breton are just simple wooden structures. In Russia, throngs of people toured through the old churches as if they were nothing more than mausoleums housing the remains of an old-fashioned worldview and way of life. Where I live, abandoned churches seem to have no historical value at all; they simply crumble and decay as they await the possibility of being converted to another purpose.

During a visit to one of the largest prisons in South Africa, I visited the prison museum, which was located next door. As interesting as it was to see the old implements used to restrain the prisoners, and to learn about the harsh and archaic methods used to punish them, I couldn't help wondering why so many people are more interested in visiting the prison museum than visiting the lonely and needy prisoners right next door.

There is no doubt that a good museum provides people with an interesting educational experience. Our little museum is like that and those responsible for its operation are doing a superb job of engaging the community in understanding and celebrating the culture of previous generations. In fact the museum is emerging as a focal place in the life of the community. There is more interest, more engagement, and more activism among people related to the museum than there is among people related to the churches.

Churches, which have historically been living communities of faith, are being abandoned while the museum housing the remains of the past is coming alive. There is something terribly wrong when museums bring life into a community while churches become relics of religious faith no longer connected to real life and the needs of the community.

The museum isn't about making history, it is about preserving and conserving the artifacts and details of history. The church, on the other hand, should be a history-making, life-infusing community of people who celebrate the life of Jesus in worship and in service by embracing the needy and the marginalized, and provide welcome, refuge and support for all people.

I find myself standing between the museum and the old white church. I'd love to see the church once again become the living embodiment of Jesus' presence, engaging exciting and building the cultural, moral, and spiritual life of our community, something that the museum can never do. But this isn't just about buildings or institutions; it is about those of us who follow Jesus wherever we are. It is a question of relevance. Is our faith really the living expression of Jesus in everyday life or is it more like a museum artifact or a nostalgic memory?

We are all bonded into one body, the body of humanity, which ever since the Word became flesh and one of us, is the body of Christ. We are called together in love and in compassion to be a witness and a sign of the waters flowing from the heart of God, calling all of humanity to the eternal wedding feast of Love.[1]

---

1 (Jean Vanier, *Community and Growth (revised edition)*; New York, Paulist Press 1989—page 103).

CHAPTER 5

ALL SAINTS' HOTEL

"Church," spat the agitated woman I was speaking with, "is not for me. It's full of hypocrites."

"Well, I can't argue with you on that," I responded. "All I know is that it is awfully difficult for me to really live like Jesus taught. Even St Paul admitted that he often found himself doing things he knew were wrong and not doing the things he knew were right. Even the disciples of Jesus were hypocritical. St Peter and the others vowed to stick with Jesus through thick and thin but then abandoned him in the face of trouble."

"Think about Mother Theresa," I continued, "she struggled immensely with doubt. She may not have looked like a hypocrite because she gave herself so completely to serving the poorest of the poor, but she actually had difficulty connecting all the dots in her faith and often felt like a hypocrite."

I will be the first to admit that there are some real hypocrites in the Church. I am part of the Church and there are often times when I mess up. If you look at my life, it won't take you long to see the traces of anger, prejudice, selfishness, and pride. The problem is not that the Church is full of hypocrites, but that we Church people often give the impression that we are better than those outside the Church. Like the Pharisee in Luke 18:9-14, we are often smug about our spirituality and faith in comparison to non-believers, or people of non-Christian religions, and "obvious sinners."

Each year Christians in some traditions celebrate a special day known as "All Saints Day." It has been celebrated at various times of the year since the second century, to commemorate the lives of martyrs throughout the ages who died because of their faith—to celebrate the lives of believers who lived extraordinary, exemplary lives. While some Christian traditions have recognized certain people as saints, spiritual "perfection" itself is not a prerequisite for membership in the Church. In truth, every saint has a history and some of their histories range from the sinful and the sordid to the sorrowful and sublime. More significant for the Church than the stories of these saints is the belief that every sinner in the world has a future.

The Church exists to encourage, motivate, and support sinners in discovering that they are actually the beloved sons and daughters of the Heavenly Father. Because of that, they have a hope and a future that is far beyond the disaster of their lives.

As Christians we are recovering sinners learning to walk in the way of Jesus, the Church should never be seen as a hotel for saints, but should rather be a hospital for sinners. It is a place where people come for hope, help, and healing. The Church will always be full of hypocrites, people who are struggling on their way to becoming fully and finally healed of sin. Nobody needs to be a good person as a prerequisite to be in the Church. The problem is that many of us in the Church aren't honest about our own continuing struggles and imperfections. So it seems as though the Church is an exclusive holy club, All Saints Hotel, hovering somewhere above the real world.

Churches are a reflection of our values and attitudes. When churches function more like exclusive hotels than rehabilitation centers they cease to be real and relevant to the community. Eventually they become just another artifact of what once was and of what could have been.

CHAPTER 6

SO WHO DO YOU THINK YOU ARE!?

66 Just who the xxxx do you think you are?" yelled the shopkeeper, for no apparent reason. Startled by his aggressive outburst, I backed away, careful not to incite him to further anger.

I don't really know what set him off—possibly there was something in my attitude or demeanor that triggered his outburst. I had only been inside the shop for a few minutes and had been examining a small sculpture to see if it was a genuine work of art or just one of many mass-produced trinkets created in some foreign factory. Who do I really think I am, I wondered, as I retreated from the shop, and what do I think of myself?

I remember being told by my mother that "you are what you eat," as she tried coaxing me into healthier eating habits and away from junk foods. If, in some way, I am what I eat, then I must also be what I think. Perhaps this is even truer than I realized. Didn't Jesus challenge the Pharisees with the idea that it is not what people eat that makes them spiritually unclean but that spiritual contamination emanates from their hearts. The question of who I think I am might well begin with, What do I think about? Inevitably our values, attitudes, and behaviors reflect our true character.

The Secret, a popular book of several years ago, purports to reveal a long-hidden law of the universe that success, growth, and well-being are directly related to positive mental energy. By the "Law of Attraction" people whose minds are given to thinking positive thoughts about something that they desire will attract positive results and will achieve or receive according to their positive and unwavering thoughts.

While the power of positive thinking is undeniable, there is no law of the universe that guarantees positive results. If there were such a law, then I know a few people who would be millionaires today instead of bankrupt dreamers. However, it is true that our thoughts shape who we are. Our words, attitude and behavior reflect the content and direction of our thoughts. I know many criminals who never dreamed of being sent to prison, but the schemes and greed that took root in their minds eventually found expression in the behavior that got them into trouble.

Our deepest thoughts give shape and direction to who we are. If I think constantly about work, I will exhibit the traits of being a workaholic. If I am preoccupied with money and success, my life will become defined by the pursuit of wealth and tinged with greed. If my thoughts are obsessed with sex, my life will become captive to lust. If my thoughts are all about me and my needs, I will become a self-absorbed and selfish person. If my thoughts are centered increasingly on Christ and His kingdom, my life will reflect the presence of Christ and the values of His kingdom.

So who do you think you are? This is a question that can best be answered by examining the things that occupy our thoughts. You and I live in the direction and the substance of our thoughts; our innermost aspirations, our secret dreams, and the things we really treasure most.

"... the things that come out of the mouth come from the heart, and these make a man 'unclean.' For out of the heart come evil thoughts, murder, adultery, sexual immorality, theft, false testimony, slander. These are what make a man 'unclean'..." (Matt. 15:18-20).

"Almighty God, to you all hearts are open, all desires known, and from you no secrets are hid: Cleanse the thoughts of our hearts by the inspiration of your Holy Spirit, that we may perfectly love you, and worthily magnify your holy Name; through Christ our Lord. Amen" (Book of Common Prayer, Anglican).

CHAPTER 7

ON BEING TREASURE HUNTERS

A southeast wind had been blowing steadily off the coast for nearly three days and by the evening of day three it was predicted to reach gale force. Known in our area as a "souete," this gale-force wind is usually accompanied by heavy rainfall and reduced visibility. Out on the sea, waves build into white-frothed, rolling mountains of water, making travel by ship both uncomfortable and very treacherous. The rugged coastline of northern Cape Breton Island bears testament to that danger and is littered with shipwrecks and stories of treasures lost and yet to be discovered.

I have watched divers methodically scouring the seabed of Aspy Bay searching for the wreckage of the *Auguste*, a merchant sailing ship that foundered and sank there during a violent storm in 1761. For more than two hundred years treasure hunters have searched for the lost treasure accompanying the 121 wealthy passengers who are known to have been aboard the *Auguste*. To date, several of her cannons and other noteworthy artifacts, including gold and silver coins, have been recovered. The main treasure trove that was reportedly stowed in barrels at the stern of the ship remains lost.

I listened to one modern-day treasure hunter telling his story of searching for the lost bounty of the *Auguste*. Even as he talked about the expense of his quest, the use of modern technology and the laborious process of an underwater search, his eyes gleamed with passion and hope. "I know it's only a matter of time and cost," he said. "But the treasure is there somewhere beneath the shifting sand on the bottom of the bay."

The romantic notion of discovering a long-lost treasure has captivated my imagination since I was a child. In the economic conditions of today, the idea of finding a treasure like that is enormously appealing. I will admit that from time to time, in reverie, as I walk along the shore I imagine myself stumbling upon a broken barrel, spilling with time-encrusted golden coins and seaweed. Treasure found ... and it's all mine! But when I return, the daily mail arrives and the bills that I need to pay cannot be paid with dreams.

It is far easier to fantasize about finding treasure and fortunes than it is to actually be a serious treasure hunter. As I listened to the treasure hunter speak, and as I read his stories, it becomes very clear to me that real treasure hunters are men and women whose focus in life and driving passion is to find treasure. They are willing to risk everything to find that treasure and for many of them it is a life-long, honest quest. That is what their lives are all about and they are not distracted by discoveries of trash or trinkets in the sand. It is the treasure trove that really matters.

Jesus spoke of the kingdom of heaven as being a treasure that can be found. It is a treasure trove of such great value that anyone who discovers it gives up everything in order to possess it; a treasure that becomes a driving passion and a defining possession. In a very real sense followers of Jesus are men and women whose lives are bent on discovering the kingdom of God, treasure hunters whose passion is reflected in what they value and how they spend their time.

> *"The kingdom of heaven is like treasure hidden in a field. When a man found it, he hid it again, and then in his joy went and sold all he had and bought that field. Again, the kingdom of heaven is like a merchant looking for fine pearls. When he found one of great value, he went away and sold everything he had and bought it"* (Matt. 13:44-46).

Part B

Beyond Criticism: Living Graciously in a Judgmental World

———❖———

CHAPTER 8

RUSHING FROM DISASTER
INTO JUDGMENT

"**H**ave you even read the book?" thundered the outraged television comedian. "Out of all the things in the Bible you could draw on to give comfort and hope to people caught in this terrible tragedy you choose [judgment]!"[1] He was reacting to statements made by a well-known American evangelist who said that the devastating earthquake was God's punishment on Haiti for the supposed pact made by Haitian leaders with the devil more than two hundred years ago.

As I watched televised images of destruction and disaster unfold before my eyes and heard cries of anguished desperation, I felt sickened to the core. Even with a massive emergency response under way, help was too late in coming for hundreds of people with crushing injuries. Yet amid scenes of death and desperation, I saw groups of Haitians praying and singing on the broken, rubble-choked streets, praising the Lord as their "ever-present help in time of trouble" (Psalm 46:1). As tears came to my eyes, I felt a growing sense of indignation at those who were rushing into

---

1 Jon Stewart on the *Daily Show* Comedy Central 14 January 2010—USA.

judgment instead of rushing into mercy. God, for sure, does not hate the suffering Haitian people and does not distance Himself from them in their time of tragedy and trouble.

Amid the unimaginable spectacle of devastation, I also saw images of the collapsed National Penitentiary. With a capacity for 1,000 prisoners, in the days just prior to the earthquake, there were nearly 4,000 prisoners jammed into the prison. Small cells designed for twelve prisoners held as many as seventy who were confined for up to twenty-three hours a day without running water or proper toilets. Excrement was tossed outside or into the gutters in the corridor. The penitentiary was reported [2] as being dangerously overcrowded—a powder keg—with rampant abuse and high rates of preventable diseases. But there are many who say that when prisoners suffer they are simply getting what they deserve.

When the earthquake struck, miraculously very few of the prisoners were killed or seriously injured. With walls collapsing around them, and steel bars breaking apart, they found freedom from their miserable world only to exit into another world of misery and disaster. I don't know what has become of the thousands of prisoners who found unexpected freedom following the earthquake, but I suspect that their experience will only magnify what most inmates experience when they exit their prison ordeal.

The reality is that the imprisonment of people results in social and moral disaster. Even under relatively good prison conditions, the forcible confinement of human beings does

2   Pulitzer Center, May 2008.

not produce good results. Around the world between 60 to 70 percent of those in prison have either been in prison previously or will reoffend after they are released.

Prison does not make bad men good. Research proves that the longer persons are imprisoned the more likely they are to reoffend after release. One reason for this is that when inmates are finally freed from prison, they exit into the disaster of homelessness, unemployment, broken families, social rejection, and an environment they may no longer recognize or relate to.

There are some who say that people in prison deserve what they get, that imprisonment is justice, and that it represents God's judgment on their complicity in evil. Some rush into judging offenders and ex-prisoners as being unworthy human beings. But Jesus didn't do that. He said that He came to proclaim freedom to the prisoners and to release the oppressed; that He came for the morally and spiritually sick, not for the healthy (Mark 2:17), and that when we treat prisoners with compassion we are actually visiting our compassion on Jesus (Matt. 25:31-46). St Paul, who also found unexpected release from prison when an earthquake rocked its stone foundations and broke the chains that shackled him (Acts 16:26), left a mighty challenge to his fellow believers. "Remember those in prison as if you were their fellow-prisoners, and those who are ill-treated as if you yourselves were suffering" (Heb. 13:3).

Rushing into judgment is a way of avoiding responsibility; it is a way of escaping from caring, a way out of compassion, grace, and love. Of course, we can see that many offenders suffer the logical consequences of bad decisions and actions, but it does not help us or them to focus only on their fault and on judgment. When a person's wrongful ways and guilt are obvious, it is so much easier to go with the flow of criticism against them than to resist that flow with the love and grace of God.

> *"Do not judge, and you will not be judged. Do not condemn, and you will not be condemned. Forgive, and you will be forgiven. Give, and it will be given to you. A good measure, pressed down, shaken together and running over, will be poured into your lap. For with the measure you use, it will be measured to you"* (Luke 6:37-38).

CHAPTER 9

CRITIC'S CHOICE

"Now, that is a sloppy way to tack a boat, a spectacle of incompetence," I said, pointing to a nearby sailboat with its sails flopping in the wind as the captain attempted to turn. It didn't cross my mind that just minutes ago I had made a somewhat similar spectacle of myself. Of course, I knew the reasons why my attempt had gone wrong ... it was a sudden wind shift as I came around the headland. But I gave no such excuse for the other sailor. "His problem," I pronounced with a sense of authority and superiority, "is inexperience, poor seamanship. If he had only been watching the wind patterns on the water, he could have anticipated the shift and timed his move accordingly ..."

For a few moments I felt a kind of satisfaction for having witnessed another sailor's poor performance. Somehow criticizing him made me feel better about myself, taking the focus off my embarrassment for my own sloppy maneuver. Criticism does that, doesn't it? Drawing attention to the failures and quirks of others seems to deflect attention from our own shortcomings. To be a critic is to rise above the masses as though one is an authority on what is good and what is not. Critics are in a class by themselves, professionals who make their living by evaluating and publicly commenting on their fields of focus.

Like many people I tend to pay close attention to what those critics say. If a particular book is described in disparaging terms, I will probably not be inclined to read it and less inclined to purchase it. When a vintage is characterized as having a vegetal aftertaste, I will not risk serving it to our dinner guests. And when a performance is described as being lackluster rather than sparkling, I will not buy a ticket even if the price is reasonable. Critics are regarded as authorities in their field views and can be trusted to discern what is good and what is less than good. The words and views of critics influence choices and perspectives. Yet I have seldom, if ever, met a professional critic who is actually an accomplished writer, performer, artist, or winemaker. They make their living as critics not as real artists or artisans.

Criticism has become regarded as a normal and necessary part of our social environment. It is a way of life. We consume criticism and become adept at offering our own, considering ourselves discerning, especially when it pertains to people and their behavior. As a person who visits prisons and prisoners all over the world, I have never thought of myself as being particularly judgmental. Rather, I've rationalized myself as being an astute observer and commentator on life and people.

But when I read what Jesus said about criticism, I try to be conscious of my tendency toward critical observation and comment. All too often the realization comes too late as I become acutely aware of how my day is peppered with

47

critical thoughts and all too frequent, negative comments about other people.

How can I possibly be a conduit of God's grace and an extension of His divine embrace, love, and mercy in this judgmental world if I am constantly finding fault with, and criticizing, the shortcomings of others? Such a negative mindset is a disgrace, the antithesis of One who came into the world not to criticize (judge) the rough ways of fishermen, the extravagance of business moguls, the corruption of tax collectors, the immorality of easy women or the men who use them, the pride and prejudice of politicians, or the swagger of soldiers and enforcers, but as the One who came to live and die as an act of love and forgiveness for all manner of people (John 12:47). It strikes me that the very people we tend to criticize are the focus of the Savior's outstretched, wounded arms.

It is so easy to point our fingers at the people who don't measure up to our expectations, and even easier to vilify those who are quite repugnant. Yet neither they nor we become better persons for our having done so.

Lord be merciful to me a critic.

"Do not judge, and you will not be judged.
Do not condemn, and you will not be condemned.
Forgive, and you will be forgiven.
Give, and it will be given to you.
A good measure, pressed down, shaken together and
*   running over, will be poured into your lap.*
For with the measure you use, it will be measured to
*   you ...*

Why do you look at the speck of sawdust in your
brother's eye
and pay no attention to the plank in your own eye?"
(Luke 6:37-38, 41)

CHAPTER 10

BETWEEN CONDEMNATION
AND COMPASSION

Sometimes I find myself impaled on the horns of a dilemma. As I walk among imprisoned men and women who are suffering, I ache with compassion and solidarity in their misery, incensed by heartless powers that degrade living human beings. I cry out for justice to be served.

As I walk among the imprisoned, I am also aware that many of them "deserve" to be punished for they are criminals. I am revolted by the thought of those who have raped their own little children; murdered innocent people without thinking; perverted the young, abused the elderly, and exploited the vulnerable and committed unspeakable abuses to satisfy their cravings, and I cry out for justice to be done. This is the dilemma for me: if I openly condemn the brutality of a prison system and the people in power, they will very likely prohibit me from coming into prison. As a result I will not be able to sit as a friend among the prisoners, nor will I be able to embrace them with the dignity and love of Jesus. It is a difficult situation, for if I take my place of compassion and solidarity among the imprisoned and do not condemn the corruption of the system, I will be seen by those who suffer as spineless and naïve for failing to confront the powers who perpetrate inhumanity, and I may lose the support of people who are passionate about injustice.

What did Jesus do, I often wonder, when He was confronted with a choice between compassion and condemnation? I became acutely aware of this dilemma some years ago when, after visiting the prisons of a notorious dictatorship in Latin America, I was wined and dined by the head of the prison system at his country estate. Known for being bloody and ruthless in his abuse of power, he was nevertheless a charming dinner host. Everything within me wanted to condemn him, to cry out on behalf of the voiceless and oppressed. But at the same time, I yearned to create an opening in order to somehow alleviate the suffering of the prisoners. In the end I felt compelled by Jesus to choose compassion over condemnation for the sake of the prisoners.

During visits to the Middle East, I have been painfully reminded of the excruciating choice we often face between condemnation and compassion. As I have walked among my fellow believers in Jesus who are a beleaguered minority, I have listened to them speak about their loneliness and sense of betrayal and abandonment by Christians in the West. To them, Christians in the West seem more aligned in condemning the Muslim world than in supporting their fellow Christian believers in the Middle East.

Many Christian believers have been killed by fundamentalist terrorists on account of their faith. One of the unintended consequences of Western Christian condemnation of the Muslim world is that Christian Arabs in the Middle East are seen as allies or "tools" of the West. Whenever Christians in the West put their political views and condemnation ahead of solidarity with their fellow believers in the Middle East, they inevitably contribute to their suffering.

There are more than enough people in the world to carry on the politics of condemnation. But there are all too few who suffer with Jesus in compassion for people we may not even know—whether they be prisoners, homeless, drug-addicted, poor, or our distant brothers and sisters in "enemy" countries.

What did Jesus choose, between condemnation and compassion?

Then Jesus cried out, "Those who believe in me do not believe in me only, but in the one who sent me. When they look at me, they see the one who sent me. I have come into the world as a light, so that no one who believes in me should stay in darkness. As for those who hear my words but do not keep them, I do not judge them. For I did not come to judge the world but to save the world" (John 12:44-47).

And [Jesus] sent messengers on ahead, who went into a Samaritan village to get things ready for him; but the people there did not welcome him, because he was heading for Jerusalem. When the disciples James and John saw this, they asked, "Lord do you want us to call fire down from heaven to destroy them?" But Jesus turned and rebuked them (Luke 9:52-55).

CHAPTER 11

DEATH OF A NOBODY

W ho outside of Venezuela would have even cared about the ten prisoners who were killed during a bloody uprising in La Planta prison?[1] It seems not to have mattered much at all to most people. They were only prisoners anyway, their personal identities of no real public interest, lost beneath the media's unseemly fascination with crime and violence. In any case, the death of a criminal is usually deemed good riddance.

I might well have passed over this news item myself had it not been for the fact that three of the dead prisoners had been trusted volunteers, colleagues of my friends in Prison Fellowship. Two of the men served as peer instructors in weekly workshops and discussion groups. The third man was the inmate leader of a small group of prisoners trying to follow Jesus amid the dank, overcrowded confines of La Planta's Pavilion Two.

During a recent two-year period, prison violence in Venezuela has taken a heavy toll, resulting in some eight hundred prisoners killed and nearly 1,500 wounded. So it is hardly surprising that this story was no big deal and

---

1 http://www.vheadline.com/readnews.asp?id=87960

that the dead men might just as well have been nobodies. But they were not nobodies. Each of them had a name, a family, and people who loved them. Though prisoners, three of those men were making a difference for good in a place that was notorious for its violence and corruption. None of the news reports actually mentioned the names of those men; they remained nameless nobodies. Yet, before God, labeling a man with a number, even denying his name altogether, does not reduce his intrinsic worth as a human being who is capable of doing good.

Just exactly how and why those prisoners died isn't clear. I would not be surprised to learn that they died while trying to keep the peace and protect their fellow inmates. There are many stories of compassion and heroism in prison. In 1941 a Polish prisoner, inmate number 16770, who had been charged with committing crimes against the state, was killed while trying to save a fellow prisoner's life. It happened on a day that one of his fellow inmates was missing during the evening count. Angered by the possibility of defiance and escape, the brutal guards randomly selected ten other prisoners for severe punishment in order to teach the prisoners a lesson. When one of the selected men cried out in anguish, "My wife! My children! I will never see them again," prisoner 16770 courageously stepped forward from the ragged rank of inmates and offered to take his place. The guards took him.

Recalling this experience some years later, the man whose life was spared because of prisoner number 16770 said, "I could only thank him with my eyes. I was stunned and could hardly grasp what was going on. The immensity of it. I, the condemned, am to live and someone else willingly and voluntarily offers his life for me—a stranger. Is this some dream? I was put back into my place without having had time to say anything. I was saved. And I owe to him the fact that I could tell you all this."[2] Franciszek Gajowniczek was saved by a fellow inmate, number 16770, a man with a name. He was Maximilian Kolbe, a Polish priest.

Every year during Easter, we commemorate the life of another prisoner who was among three who were sentenced to death. Two of those prisoners have remained unknown— nobodies for over two thousand years. The third prisoner was Jesus of Nazareth who, in his dying breath, offered hope and life to one of those men as he was crying out for mercy. Legend has ascribed the name Dysmas to him.

The story of Jesus, the prisoner, is a story I love telling inmates I meet in the prisons of the world. While most people in society often do not regard prisoners as worthy of respect, far less worth redeeming, Jesus gave His life for the sake of prisoners, named and unnamed, everywhere.

Prisoners aren't nobodies. Prisoners, like everyone else who is ignored and lost, have names, stories, and futures, and are immeasurably loved by the God who loves us and who calls us to love like Him.

> *... all mankind is of one author, and is one volume;*
> *when one man dies, one chapter is not torn out of the*
> *book,*

---

2   http://www.auschwitz.dk/ olbe.htm

but translated into a better language;
and every chapter must be so translated ...
God employs several translators;
some pieces are translated by age,
some by sickness, some by war, some by justice;
but God's hand is in every translation,
and his hand shall bind up all our scattered leaves
again,
for that library where every book shall lie open to one
another;
as therefore the bell that rings to a sermon,
calls not upon the preacher only,
but upon the congregation to come;
so this bell calls us all: but how much more me ... [3]

---

3   From John Donne's *'Meditation XVII' (Nunc lento sonitu dicunt, morieris.)*

CHAPTER 12

NEVER TRUST A BEGGAR

Bleary eyed, swaying unsteadily, reeking of alcohol and urine, a disheveled beggar accosted me near a streetside food kiosk. With one finger pointing to his open mouth and his other hand patting his sunken abdomen, he made it clear to me, "I am starving, give me food. I am too weak to speak." Having encountered beggars of all sorts, I have become just a bit jaded and cynical. Although I "knew" it wasn't really food he was after, I offered him the food I had just purchased. With immediate disgust, he rejected my "generosity" and scowled, belligerently thrusting his hand toward me for money.

"Never trust a beggar," I muttered under my breath, knowing that it was a heartless thing to say. Yet how often we automatically avert our eyes from the sight of a beggar sprawled on the sidewalk or beckoning between cars at stop lights? And how often we simply pass by their outstretched hands as if they don't exist? How easily we dismiss beggars because we know that what we give will only be used for drink or drugs or smokes? The beggars' stories, like their pleas, cannot be trusted and I for one do not appreciate being manipulated and refuse to contribute to their decadence.

Of course, I have met a few legitimate beggars who simply are so down on their luck that they have no alternative but to throw themselves on the mercy of passers-by who can't say no, passers-by who actually feel good about themselves for tossing a few coins their way. More often than not I am one of those. On some occasions I even stop to look a beggar in the eye and listen to his story, while deep within my cynical mind I actually don't believe a word of it. In my own mind I am saying, "Get a job. Get up off your butt. Get real. Be honest. You're a loser and a user!"

Somehow, I can't escape the feeling of being complicit in the charade of beggarly dishonesty, whether I half-heartedly respond to the false appeal or even pause to hear a tale of woe. A question lingers in my mind . Should I give to beggars even when I know that what I give will be misused for alcohol or drugs and not for food or coffee, or even for the medicine for their sick children? Wouldn't I have more integrity by just saying no?

Recently, a good friend told me about a man who responded to an appeal by making a very substantial donation to a charitable organization. After some time it was discovered that the charity had used the donation for a completely different and rather questionable purpose. "Knowing that your donation was abused, do you have any regrets about what you did? Would you take your donation back if you could?" asked my friend. "No," he replied. "What I gave, I gave to God not to the organization. What people do with it is not my problem; it is on their conscience before God."

It is not just street people who are begging, it is also organizations who beg on behalf of others. As we are confronted by the beggars and the needy of the world, we all have to learn the lesson of giving as though we are giving directly to God, who loves the beggar regardless of his condition or motivation. Does that mean I don't see the beggar as a real person, or that I am abdicating my own responsibility to be a good steward? On the contrary, I think I respect the beggar all the more by not imposing my cynicism or distrusting his intentions.

Perhaps there is a spirituality in giving to beggars without condition, a spirituality found in what Jesus really meant when He said, "For I was hungry and you gave me something to eat, ... I was in prison and you came to visit me" (Matt. 25:35, 36). In giving to the beggar or visiting the prisoner, you and I entrust ourselves and what we give to God. I am coming to believe that Jesus sometimes comes to us in the disguise of beggars who revolt us.

> *Jesus is my God,*
> *Jesus is my Spouse,*
> *Jesus is my Life,*
> *Jesus is my only Love,*
> *Jesus is my All in All;*
> *Jesus is my Everything*
> *The dying, the cripple, the mental,*
> *the unwanted, the unloved*
> *they are Jesus in disguise.*
>
> (Mother Theresa of Calcutta)

CHAPTER 13

JUST TRUST ME

To be trusted is a greater compliment than to be loved. [1]

"Trust but verify" was the memorable and pithy phrase often used by former US President Ronald Reagan in his dealings with Cold War leaders of the Soviet Union. Ironically, the phrase mirrored a well-known Russian proverb [2] that had been a favorite saying of Felix Dzerzhinsky, [3] the ruthless founder and director of the Bolshevik Secret Police. [4]

Among the mementos I've kept from my early involvement within the Soviet prison system is a carved portrait of Dzerzhinsky given to me by a journalist who told me the story behind the portrait that had been given to him by an elderly former political prisoner. He was an artist, considered dissident, who had experienced torture and deprivation at the hands of the KGB in the notorious Lubyanka Prison in Moscow. The Lubyanka Prison regime was cal-

---

1   George MacDonald, (*The Marquis of Lossie* 1877, chapter 4).

2   A translation of the Russian proverb *"doveryai, no proveryai"* (Доверяй, но проверяй).

3   1877-1926.

4   Cheka—later known as the OGPU, NKGB, MGB and then KGB from 1954 until the break-up of the Soviet Union.

culated to breed distrust and fear. "Nobody trusted me," the prisoner said. "We prisoners didn't trust each other and the guards couldn't even trust each other." So in that milieu of suspicion and fear the prisoner devised a plan to avoid torture and possible execution by carving a portrait of the man revered and feared as the "father" of the KGB.

"I am doing this for our leader, Dzerzhinsky," the prisoner would tell the guards as he slowly and painstakingly etched the likeness from memory. Not knowing if the prisoner had actually been a friend of Dzerzhinsky or not, and being afraid to verify his story for fear of reprisal, the guards simply let him be. While they couldn't trust, they didn't verify and therefore avoided doing him harm for fear of interfering with "Dzerzhinsky's artist." The portraiture bought the prisoner enough time to gain his release from prison. When he was discharged, he took the carving with him.

"I don't trust nobody," is a phrase I often hear among prisoners. "I've gotta look out for myself because nobody else will." In a world of trust betrayed and trust misplaced, it is little wonder that the phrase "trust me" begs for proof. Amid stories of financial scandal involving billions of dollars, investors no longer trust that their "trust accounts" are secure with investment managers. In a culture where a promise is only a promise until things change, marriage vows of love and fidelity, "till death do us part," fail in the face of fatal attractions and distractions. When political leaders knowingly promise things they cannot deliver, the trust of people in government gives way to cynicism that undermines the foundations of communities and nations.

"In God we Trust" states the denominated currency of America, and yet people are disappointed both in the stock market and in God for not improving the economy. It is admittedly difficult to trust God, not only when people lose their jobs, but when terrible calamities overtake decent hard-working people. And even for people of faith, trust is put at risk when the lives of those who claim to know and speak for God betray the moral values and spiritual truth they espouse.

"Just trust me," I remember saying to a frightened young delinquent boy standing on the edge of a cliff during a rock-climbing exercise designed to build confidence and trust. "I am holding the rope, and I won't let you fall."

"It's not you," he said in a quivering voice, "I'm scared. I can't do it. What if the rope breaks?"

"Trust me, this rope won't break. You've already seen the other guys do it," I responded, trying to allay his unfounded fears. But he never did make the climb; his trust in me and in himself was insufficient. I had known it would be difficult for him; everything he had experienced in his short life was about betrayal and disappointment. He was an unwanted, unloved kid from a tragically broken and abusive home. He fared no better living on the streets as a runaway as all too often his would-be benefactors demanded sex in exchange for food and money. In protective foster care he quickly learned that he wasn't part of a real family. Because he felt like a project, he didn't trust his guardians and turned to drugs and petty thieving until he was arrested.

There is so little hope for a kid living in a society where "you can't trust no one." Prisons are a magnifying mirror of what is wrong in society, says British criminologist Baroness Vivien Stern. In a "trust but verify" world, trust is no longer trust. When kids in trouble grow up to inhabit the prisons of the world, it is not just their problem, it is a symptom of a deepening problem in society. And if individuals cannot trust the people they live with, how will they ever learn to trust God whom they cannot see?

One of the painful lessons I've had to learn, and am still learning, is to mean what I say and to do what I say. My speaking the good words of the gospel, and pointing people to the God who can be trusted falls on deaf ears if I am not trustworthy. The good news of grace will be trusted by people only to the extent that I am gracious and trustworthy in my relationships with them. In a world of cynicism and mistrust, a good messenger is one whose life verifies the message of God's trustworthy love.

"Again, you have heard that it was said to the people long ago, 'Do not break your oath, but keep the oaths you have made to the Lord.' But I tell you, Do not swear at all: either by heaven, for it is God's throne; or by the earth, for it is his footstool; or by Jerusalem, for it is the city of the Great King. And do not swear by your head, for you cannot make even one hair white or black. Simply let your 'Yes' be 'Yes' and your 'No,' 'No'; anything beyond this comes from the evil one" (Matt. 5:33-37 NIV).

63

CHAPTER 14

IT'S THE HONEST TRUTH

It was more than just a look of incredulity; it was obvious that my friend didn't believe a word I was saying. "But, it's the honest truth. I swear it is," I persisted. Whether I had given him prior reason to disbelieve me or not, I don't know, but the fact is that he was not taking my words at face value. I understand, for I tend not to take things at face value when attestations and protestations of truth feel incongruent with my expectations.

In the Western world persons appearing before a court of law are "sworn in" prior to giving testimony. Under oath and penalty of perjury they declare to tell "the truth, the whole truth, and nothing but the truth." I've always wondered why we don't just settle for telling the truth. Why does the telling of truth need to be hedged with the addition of "the whole truth" and "nothing but the truth"?

I suppose it is because the pure and simple truth is not always what is spoken and, for many people, truth is often tailored to fit their needs and self-interest. In order to enhance the believability of words, we seek some assurance that it is not just a convenient, partial truth, that it is nothing other than the unadulterated, unembellished, unaltered and un-nuanced truth. In other words, we want it to be the honest truth. But, can anything be essentially true if it isn't honest in the first place? Truth often becomes subverted when people value the convenience of being able to replace uncomfortable truth with utilitarian fabrication. After all, the truth often hurts, and it feels so much better when the truth is modified just a bit in order to be more palatable, pleasing, and acceptable.

Often it doesn't take much effort to "dress up" the truth. In a recent conversation with a colleague, we remarked on the tendency of a mutual acquaintance to embellish and exaggerate accounts of his experiences in order to make a good story even more exciting. The problem is that his stories are not the truth, the whole truth, and nothing but the truth. He doesn't present the honest truth. Instead his stories are caricatures of reality.

An American political candidate was caught embellishing an experience, the telling of which was far from the real truth. When called to account, it was reported that she had simply misspoken. According to her representative, the candidate had not really told an untruth; it was simply a "slip of speech," she had misspoken!

I really shouldn't be too critical of people who play with the truth as if I have been reflecting about the honest truth and living a truth-telling life. Recently I consciously tried to go an entire day without misrepresenting or withholding the truth in any way. I failed. It is so convenient to speak partial falsehoods, to give answers that reshape the truth with half-truths and plausible lies.

The late psychiatrist, Scott Peck, proposed that evil is manifested through the persistent and accumulative denial of truth.[1] Evil masquerades as truth in disguises that are fabricated with lies. We live in times that are characterized by false promises, misleading advertising, political distortions, economic subterfuge, and interpersonal and public deception perpetrated by institutions and systems. Jesus speaks into our times, as He has spoken into the times of people before us, of our deep-seated need for truth that will set us free from bondage (John 8:32). Ultimately misspoken truth and blatant lies create a prison from which there is no escape. We make our own prisons and the cumulative consequence of our untruthful thoughts and words and actions are evil.

Jesus challenges us to be people who are characterized by truth, the truth we believe and the truth we speak and live.

"Again, you have heard that it was said to the people
> *long ago,*
>> *'Do not break your oath, but keep the oaths you have*
>> *made to the Lord.'*
> *But I tell you, do not swear at all:*
>> *either by heaven, for it is God's throne;*
>> *or by the earth, for it is his footstool;*
>> *or by Jerusalem, for it is the city of the Great King.*
> *And do not swear by your head for you cannot make*
>> *even one hair white or black.*

---

1 *People of the Lie* by Scott Peck (Simon & Schuster, New York; 1983).

Simply let your 'Yes' be 'Yes,'
* and your 'No,' 'No';*
anything beyond this comes from the evil one."

(Matt. 5:33-37)

CHAPTER 15

THE SHAPE OF TRUTH

*Enough is enough! How much more can all of us take? Like
you, my heart is broken, my mind is confused, my body
hurts and I have moved in and out of a variety of feelings,
especially shame and frustration, fear and disappointment,
along with a sense of vulnerability, and a tremendous
poverty of spirit. I have cried and I have silently screamed,
and perhaps that was my prayer to God: Why Lord? What
does all this mean? What do you want to see happen among
your people? ... Are people going to stop believing, will
faithful people stop being people of faith?* [1]

My innermost being resonated with this deep cry of
anguish as newspaper headlines screamed "Bishop
Busted,"[2] the Roman Catholic Bishop of the Antigonish
Diocese (Nova Scotia) charged with child pornography.
Bishop Lahey was a respected leader, a kind and brilliant

---

1 Excerpted from the letter of Anthony Mancini, the Archbishop of Halifax, Nova
Scotia, to *"the Roman Catholic Faithful of Nova Scotia" 2 October 2009.* http://
www.catholichalifax.org/images/stories/BishopOffice/2009%2010%2002%20
All%20RC%20of%20NS.pdf

2 *The Chronicle Herald* (Halifax, Nova Scotia) Thursday, 1 October 2009 (Page 1)
*"Bishop Busted—Lahey accused of possessing, importing sexual images of child-
ren"* by Alison Auld.

man who had just led the Roman Catholic Church through the agonizing process of settling claims brought by sexual abuse victims against the Church and some of her priests. And after going through all of that, now this? Enough is indeed enough of the pain and embarrassment inflicted on individuals and communities by leaders whose lives betray the truth, when the dross of things they thought were private sees the light of day.

Why are we seeing so many leaders in our churches and religious organizations fail? Perhaps they are just more visible than other folks, or perhaps they are just subjected to more pressures. Clearly, sexual dalliance and deviance are not just evidenced among Roman Catholic priests. This is also a problem among single and married: Protestant, evangelical, and charismatic leaders, as well as Roman Catholics.

Within days of hearing the news about Bishop Lahey, I happened to see a news clip in which a popular American television personality publicly admitted to having had sexual relationships with women on his staff. The audience laughed as he cleverly divulged that information. It was hard to tell if the audience really thought his infidelities were humorous, or if he was deliberately making a joke of those affairs in order to cover up his own public embarrassment.[3] Perhaps it was a bit of both, but as I watched I couldn't help but feel sorry for his wife and family who probably find no humor, intended or otherwise, in his affairs with other women

---

3   David Letterman of CBS *The Late Show*.

In the news during the same week was the arrest, in Switzerland, of Roman Polanski, the celebrated Polish-French film director.[4] Based on criminal charges dating back more than thirty years, Mr Polanski was detained by Swiss police for possible extradition to the United States on charges of having taken sexual advantage of a very young girl. Although the victim has long since expressed her forgiveness, Polanski faced the very real possibility of "paying the price" for the sins of his past. While undoubtedly there were those who will find satisfaction in a "forgiven" old man being held to account, I wondered what satisfaction there would be for the old man and for the girl when all is said and done.

I ponder what meaning there was in these three disparate stories. In a way, all three men are leaders who betrayed public trust and are having to face the consequences of their actions. But there is no real news in that. Perhaps the real news is that their private lives are ultimately not as private as they hoped or as they had intended. I often think about the moral responsibility that leaders have for their direct and indirect influence on others. Of all people in leadership, Christian leaders should be persons whose lives are shaped by the truth of their convictions and beliefs. While there is no higher moral standard for leaders in the Church than for leaders in any other field; and while there is no higher moral standard for leaders than for any other people, those of us who purport to teach and lead

---

4   http://www.nytimes.com/2009/09/28/movies/28polanski.html?_r=1&pagewanted=2

others in the way of truth have an enormous moral and spiritual responsibility to live truth-shaped lives. We are held to high account because there is no private morality that is not inextricably connected to who we are as followers of Jesus. Nothing we are and nothing we do is so personal that it may not have public consequences, no matter how good we think we look.

It is a constant challenge to live as true in private as in public. Yet we know that even if we should fail or fall, there is no disgrace beyond the reach of God's redemptive, healing grace. The shape of the truth about you and me is evidenced, not in what we say we publicly believe or teach, but by what we do in private when we think our actions are hidden from display.

Our faith in Jesus Christ is a response from the heart, a heart which has known the healing grace of mercy and forgiveness. At this time when so many hearts have been broken, we need to know again, or for the first time, the healing grace of God's love. Such healing grace can only come from all of us sharing together our faith and convictions that, in spite of sin in all its forms, mercy is stronger than anger, forgiveness is more powerful than rejection, and reconciliation is more transformative of spiritual devastation into new life possibilities.[5]

---

5   Excerpted from the letter of Anthony Mancini, the Archbishop of Halifax, Nova Scotia, to *"the Roman Catholic Faithful of Nova Scotia"* October 2, 2009.

Part C

Holy Fools: Being Light in Dismal Places

————◆————

CHAPTER 16

TABLE COMPANIONS

Who do you usually eat with? Who are the people you most look forward to inviting to your home for a fine meal?

Something dynamic happens when people come together around a table to eat, drink, and share their stories. Elias Jabbour, a Palestinian peacemaker, once told me that the greatest satisfaction of his life is seeing blood enemies put aside their enmity to sit together around a table and share a meal. In turning aside from their anger and revenge in order to eat with each other, enemies recognize their shared humanity and their common dependence for living.

Many of the stories about Jesus are set around the meals He shared with His close disciples and friends, as well as strangers from beyond the circles of religious and moral respectability. When He was criticized for including sinners among His table companions, Jesus made it clear that God's table is set to include the poor, the sick, and the unsavory, not only those within the circle of respectability. Jesus described the Kingdom of God as being like a wedding banquet in which the guests include a motley assortment of people invited, not just from the main streets, but also from the side streets and alleyways of life (Luke 14:15-24).

At the very end of His life, as Jesus shared a final meal with His companions, He was fully aware that one of them was untrustworthy and disloyal. Nevertheless, he along with the others is one of Jesus' chosen table companions. Before the meal Jesus graciously washed their feet and at the table He served them bread and wine, as representing His body and blood, spiritual food for their journey, and a foretaste of the heavenly banquet of God's Kingdom.

In the fast-food, eat-and-run culture of the Western world we have largely lost the sociability and significance of table companionship, of sharing our lives around the table of God's provision, friendship, and convivial togetherness. So often we eat quickly and alone without savoring either food or friendship. And our tables, even when they aren't set for one, are open to a guest list that generally does not extend to people who are outside our circle of family and friends.

One of the fondest memories from my youth is of my mother's hospitality toward strangers. She made certain that our table was always open to people passing through our town, whatever their nationality, beliefs, or social status. I was always amazed how sharing a meal with these people led to friendship. It was a socially enriching, intellectually stimulating, and often deeply spiritual experience for our family.

I think about table companionship, reconciliation, and spiritual nourishment as I read the familiar gospel story about the rich man who ate sumptuously every day while a poor and hungry man named Lazarus languished just outside his door (Luke 16:19-31). As I shake my head at the rich man's folly for not inviting poor Lazarus to join him at his table, my thoughts are drawn to the people with whom we typically don't share our tables. I wonder what would happen if you and I were to eat and drink with lonely ex-prisoners, elderly people who have no family, our foreign neighbors, or the folks who are socially different or "beneath" us? What would happen in our communities and the world if followers of Jesus opened their tables to Muslims and gay people, to the poor and homeless? What would happen to us? What would happen to them? Who are the people outside the doors of our hospitality, people who need to be included at our table, God's table?

Whom we include at our table makes a big difference in the world!

CHAPTER 17

BUT THEY AREN'T EVEN CHRISTIANS

I read a story in the newspaper about an American pastor who was serving in a European church during World War II.[1] With Christmas approaching, his congregation back in the United States took up a collection in order to help him come home for the holiday. As time passed and the pastor had not returned home as expected, an urgent message was sent to find out if he was experiencing some difficulty. When the pastor finally responded, he confessed that instead of using the money for himself, he had spent it helping a group of beleaguered Jews escape from the Nazis. Disappointed and chagrined by his response, they sent back a terse message, "but they aren't even Christians!"

The congregation's response reminded me of St Peter's noonday vision. While he was praying on a rooftop, he saw a sheet containing all kinds of animals and reptiles being let down from heaven, and then heard a voice saying to him, "Get up Peter, kill and eat!" He felt completely revolted by the message for the animals he saw were not at all kosher and the very thought of eating unclean animals

---

1 *Washington Post, Religion Section* (January 12, 2007).

went against every grain of his religious conviction as a Jew. What could such a bizarre vision from heaven mean?

Even as Peter pondered this question, a message came inviting him to meet with Cornelius, a Gentile centurion. As a devout Jew, Peter knew that accepting an invitation to visit the home of a Gentile was taboo. It was a sin! I can almost feel Peter's instinctive reaction, "But he isn't even a Jew!" Yet in that very moment the meaning of the vision became clear, for the Holy Spirit told him, "Do not call anything impure that God has made clean." So Peter, the Jew, crossed over the line of his religious purity and respectability to share the good news of God's love with a Gentile, by visiting the home and enjoying the embrace of an imperial Roman military official and his family (Acts 10:9-33). The explicit and implicit religious lines we often draw are not so different from those of Peter the Jew and the Christmas Christians. We are all for reaching out to evangelize "the lost," yet often reluctant to love and embrace them as our real friends.

I live and work in a place where I feel the excruciating pain of prisoners who have been visited with hope whilst in prison but, when their time is served and they return to the community, find themselves excluded in the Church. They find themselves on the social outside looking in. I know it isn't easy to come alongside a perfect stranger with prison baggage who needs a helping hand. And there are those who say that to do so would be foolish unless the person proves himself. Yet what the world needs are "holy fools" who take such risks, people who put their religious reputations and comfort on the line to embrace prisoners, prostitutes, and others who are outside the boundaries of their Christian comfort zone.

Jesus paid no heed to the crowd or to religious taboos when He reached out in love to touch unclean lepers. And He went beyond religious convention by inviting Himself to the dinner tables of rogues, rascals, and reprobates because He loved them. Jesus transcended a cultural and religious barrier to befriend women who weren't even Jewish or morally worthy because He loved them beyond all measure. To love as Jesus loves, to embrace as God embraces, is to embrace and love without any qualification. God is love and loves all people everywhere without limitation or condition.

Dear friends,
> *let us love one another,*
> *for love comes from God.*
Everyone who loves has been born of God and knows
> *God.*
Whoever does not love does not know God,
> *because God is love.*
> *This is how God showed his love among us:*
> *He sent his one and only Son into the world*
> > *that we might live through him ...*
Dear friends,
> *since God so loved us,*
> *we also ought to love one another.*
No-one has ever seen God;
> *but if we love one another,*
> *God lives in us*
and his love is made complete in us. (1 John 4:7-9, 11-12)

CHAPTER 18

CANDLEPOWER

It was during the last night of my visit to Zimbabwe that the lights went out. While frequent, unpredictable power outages are not unusual in Zimbabwe, as in many other parts of Africa, they are most inconvenient, especially at night. I did not realize until the power went off, just how dark the night really was, how difficult it would be to find my way around, and how impossible it was to do normal things like reading or packing my suitcase. When the lights went off, total darkness prevailed.

A few minutes later, my host came up to the room with a candle. I cannot remember the last time I used a candle for anything other than providing a bit of romantic ambience for an evening dinner with my wife. Even when candles are used liturgically, they serve a symbolic significance rather than being a source of illumination. However, in the depths of that Zimbabwe night the light emanating from a single candle was truly amazing, its small flickering flame dissipating the darkness.

"Now that is candlepower," I said to myself, as I resumed packing my scattered books and belongings. From my study of physics I recalled that, in the mid-nineteenth century, candlepower was adopted as the standard of measurement for a unit of luminous intensity. Several years ago I purchased a powerful one million-candlepower search light for emergency use on my boat. Sometime later, during a dark and stormy night, that powerful light enabled me to see through the darkness and avoid colliding with a boat that had broken free from its moorings and was adrift.

I've always marveled at the power of light, but it is not the physics of candlepower that captures my imagination, rather it is the beauty and the mystery of light overcoming the darkest of dark spaces. Although I once thought of darkness as being the exact opposite of light, I now realize that it is not the opposite, but rather just the absence of light. If darkness were the opposite of light, then a greater quantity of darkness could easily overpower a lesser quantity of light. As it is, no amount of darkness can extinguish or obliterate even so little a light as a candle. In fact, a single candle has the power to dispel the darkest darkness.

During my time in Zimbabwe I experienced another kind of darkness that is inherent in the economic, political and social catastrophe of a country where masses of people live in the grip of fear, deprivation, and starvation. During the time that the situation was worsening, numerous governmental and non-governmental aid and mission agencies simply abandoned the country, allowing darkness to prevail and overtake the people. Tens of thousands of desperate people subsequently sought refuge outside Zimbabwe, while thousands more simply succumbed to the scourge of hunger, disease, and violence. As is always the case, those in prison suffered the most. They are captives, powerless to cope and powerless to flee in search of refuge.

During one visit I accompanied my colleagues to meetings with prison officials and then to a prison where I saw the candlepower of their conviction, courage, and compassion pushing back the oppressive darkness of human misery. The very fact that someone cares enough to serve "undeserving," suffering prisoners powerfully penetrates through the darkness of even the worst prison. In walking through the reeking, wretched prison with my colleagues as they touched the lives of prisoners, I saw light penetrating the night of that inhumanity and injustice. There is no darkness so dire and dense that it can extinguish the candlepower of even a single act of kindness, a look of love, a gesture of compassion, or a word of hope given in the name of Jesus.

Light makes all the difference.

"You are light for all the world.
A town that stands on a hill cannot be hidden.
When a lamp is lit,
it is not put under the meal-tub, but on the lamp stand,
where it gives light to everyone in the house.
And you, like the lamp,
must shed light among your fellows,
so that when they see the good you do,
they may give praise to your Father in heaven."

(Matt. 5:14-16 NEB)

CHAPTER 19

TO THE POWER OF ONE

The number of stars in our galaxy is calculated to be around 100 billion, or 10 to the eleventh power (10^{11}), and our galaxy is just one of 100 billion galaxies thought to comprise the visible universe. By extension, the total number of stars in the entire universe is about 10 to the twenty-second power (10^{22})—numbers that completely boggle my mind. It would take more than a lifetime just to begin counting that many stars.

Such numbers are incomprehensible to me, stretching my mind toward an unimaginable infinity. Some scientists have even compared the number of stars in the universe to the total number of grains of sand on the earth (estimated at between 10^{20} and 10^{24} grains). I cannot even begin counting the grains of sand on one end of South Harbor beach near my house. Not only would people think that I'd taken leave of my senses, but I wouldn't even know how to begin counting—with a pail or perhaps just a teaspoon.

We live in a world where numbers, big numbers, are as significant for politicians, economists, epidemiologists, evangelists, criminologists, and military strategists as they are for mathematicians and physicists. There is power in numbers. Political popularity, business success, military might, national productivity, and personal performance are measured in comparative numbers signifying growth or decline. Of course, numeric increases are not always good, as in the AIDS epidemic and crime rates. But even in these areas, the larger the numbers, the greater the attention that is paid. For if the numbers are small, the problems they quantify do not merit our concern. Small numbers are of little consequence.

During his campaign for the US presidency, Barack Obama recounted the story of his visit to a small, southern town.[1] It was a hot, humid day, and he had reached the end of a demanding schedule of media interviews and campaign appearances. He was exhausted and as he reached the final event of that grueling day, it began to rain. He found himself soaking wet, wearied to the bone, and discouraged at finding only a handful of people waiting to meet him. As he entered the room, an elderly woman began chanting, quietly at first, and then with growing intensity, "I'm fired up ... and ready to go! Fired up ... and ready go go! FIRED UP! ... AND READY TO GO!" It didn't take long before every person in the small group joined her rousing chant.

"And you know what?" Barack Obama said. "In just a few minutes, I found myself fired up and ready to go." There is power in a single voice, power in a single person to make a difference. It's the power of one.

Power is not always found in big numbers. I saw that powerfully demonstrated by two young high-school students who decided to take a stand against bullying in their

---

1   National Public Radio (US) October 5, 2007.

school. On the first day of the school year, a new student had been mercilessly harassed and ridiculed by a number of other students because he had worn a pink shirt to school.[2] Two students, David and Travis, saw the injustice and the pain. The next day they came to school wearing pink tee shirts and bringing another seventy-five pink tee shirts for other students to wear as a way of expressing their solidarity with the victim and saying "no" to the school bullies. While governments and schools across North America have spent millions of dollars in anti-bullying campaigns, nothing has captured the attention of students, or produced the kind of impact, as did the courageous and creative action of those two students. Their simple, straightforward act of solidarity inspired students throughout North America in taking a stand against bullying behavior. It began with the power of one. The power of one is not without consequence or significance. Consider how the history of the world has been shaped for good or ill by Genghis Khan, Napoleon Bonaparte, Queen Victoria, Adolf Hitler, Sigmund Freud, William Wilberforce, Martin Luther King, Pope John Paul II, and Billy Graham. Consider also the people who have shaped your life most profoundly for good or ill by a word, a look, or by an act or attitude.

It is in the power of one to have a profound and positive impact on others and to change the world. Change always begins small, with the power of one who speaks up or does something that impacts others for good. Neither you nor I

---

2 As reported September 2007 in the *Halifax Chronicle Herald* (Central Kings County Rural High School, Nova Scotia, Canada).

need majority support to do that; nor do we need big numbers in our favor in order to encourage and influence the people around us for good. Mahatma Gandhi challenged his followers and critics alike to "become the change you seek." St Paul, writing from the powerlessness and isolation of his imprisonment, left this provocative blessing, "Now to him who is able to do immeasurably more than all we ask or imagine, according to his power that is at work within us" (Eph. 3:20).

The world needs more people like the woman at the soggy, political rally and like David and Travis who are fired up and ready to go! As fearful, ridiculous, or alone as we may feel, it is in the power of one to make a difference in the world.

CHAPTER 20

THE VOICES

I heard a voice, not audibly as in someone speaking aloud, but nonetheless distinctively a voice. I heard it as clearly as if someone had been running right beside me. "You are not responsible for this mess," it said. "This is not your problem. Don't be ridiculous; you're here to run."

I was running laps around a local football field with Rescue, my Border collie companion. I was trying to get into better physical condition and I certainly didn't want to interrupt my routine by picking up the empty bottles and litter strewn about the track. I felt relieved to hear the voice absolving me of responsibility for trash that wasn't mine. "It won't make any difference anyhow; picking up those bottles won't solve the real problem." The voice was right; this was definitely not my problem. I certainly couldn't prevent footballers from leaving their empty bottles and trash behind after the next game. I continued running down the field only to hear another voice, just as clearly as the first. "But this is your community and your neighborhood, isn't it?" That is true, of course, but I also know that there are people who are paid to keep it tidy. It's their job, not mine. "Besides, you've got better things to do with your time than picking up litter," affirmed the first voice. I knew that voice was right because I had very little time left to finish my morning run, shower, get dressed, and drive to work, where I had important issues to attend to. Clearly, my responsibilities at work were substantively more important.

As I completed another lap around the littered field, I heard the second voice again. "What makes you think that you're too important to pick up a few empty bottles and take them to the rubbish bin?" Well, I don't think of myself as being too important at all; it is just that I am on a busy schedule, I've got many things to do, and haven't got time to interrupt my run.

"Good on you," said the first voice. "You won't get physically fit if you let these little things distract you from your running." And that was good advice, because I was trying to build up my endurance, and stopping to pick up litter would definitely break my routine. It takes discipline and determination to make a difference.

"Is it all about you then?" asked the second voice. That was an annoying question. What in the world do a few plastic bottles have to do with that, I wondered. Surely those empty bottles don't really have anything to do with ego, selfishness, or self-importance. Do they?

"Just one more lap to go and you are done," said the first voice. "You've done well today." I felt good about my morning run. It was exhausting but exhilarating.

"But just how well have you really done," interrupted the second voice, "if you don't pick up other people's litter?"

It is surely strange how these simple conversations in the mind sometimes go. Just when you'd like to be thinking deep spiritual thoughts or how to make ends meet financially, an empty plastic bottle carelessly tossed aside, or some other seemingly inconsequential interruption becomes a focus. Sometimes God speaks to us through these apparent distractions and puts us into a place where we have to discern His voice from the voices of self-preoccupation, self-importance, self-interest, and self-justification. And there are times when it is through simple menial acts of responsibility and care that we are confronted with an opportunity to love and serve the Lord.

Do those scattered empty bottles really matter? Are the voices merely a figment of my imagination? Does it make a difference what I do as I run my final lap around the field? Is there any power in one person picking up another person's careless litter? Finally, I gave in and, feeling like a fool, picked up as many bottles as I could and took them to the rubbish bin.

CHAPTER 21

HOLY FOOLS

A few days later I was still picking up discarded bottles during my morning run. So far no one had called me a fool, at least not to my face. However, I still felt rather foolish running around the football field carrying an armload of empty bottles. I made a point of not looking at anyone. Even though I felt embarrassed to be seen picking up other people's trash, I believed that my doing so was making a statement of responsibility. Furthermore, I thought that picking up this litter was a small way of serving the Lord. At the same time, the trash-picking routine was getting a bit tiresome as there were more bottles and trash every morning. There was no change at all in the careless behavior of the football people and I was getting tired of picking up their litter. Maybe I should have gone to another place for my morning run.

I remember reading stories about odd characters in Russian literature referred to as the "holy fools." Among many "holy fools" like St Symeon of Emesis, St Andreas of Constantinople, St Xenia of Petersburg, Blessed Feofil of the Kiev Caves, undoubtedly one of the most famous was St Basil the Blessed, to whom many miracles were attrib-uted. Yet he lived the bizarre life of a vagrant, wandering the cold winter streets of Moscow naked, mocking the fur-clad pretensions of the wealthy and elite who considered him an annoyance. Yet Basil became so revered by the oppressed working-class people in the city that when he died, he was buried next to the cathedral of the "Protection of the Mother of God," instead of the paupers' cemetery outside of the city.

Among the stories likening Basil to the Old Testament prophets was the story of his daring confrontation with Ivan the Terrible. Presenting Ivan with a bloody, raw slab of meat during the "Great Lenten Fast," Basil urged Ivan to stop fasting and eat the meat. "Why abstain from dead meat when you murder men?" he taunted.

Basil became known as a "fool for Christ" and was eventually canonized by the Russian Church. Bishop Kallistos of Diokleia describes the fool for Christ as having no possessions, no family, no position, and so is able to speak with a prophetic boldness. He cannot be exploited or used by men, for he has no ambition and fears God alone. Holy fools visibly and prophetically live out the "hard-sayings" of Jesus by confronting the falseness, the hypocrisy, and the evils of society by their shocking and dramatic actions.

"Holy fools shout out with their mad words and deeds that to seek God is not necessarily the same thing as to seek sanity. We need to think long and hard about sanity, a word most of us cling to with a steel grip. Does fear of being regarded by others as insane confine me in a cage of 'responsible' behavior that limits my freedom and cripples my ability to love?"[1]

---

1   Jim Forest.

I will have to admit that respectability means a lot to me. I don't want to look like a fool, sound like a fool, or act like a fool. Nothing hurts more than to have my rationality, sensibility, and personal stability called into question. There are situations when I hesitate bowing my head for grace in a public place for fear of being thought of as a mindless religious fundamentalist. And there are other ways in which I disguise the "foolishness" of my faith.

Picking up discarded bottles day after day is really not such a big deal. After all, even if I feel foolish for doing so, I can make a rational environmental or social responsibility case to explain my behavior. There is no "holy foolishness" in that. But what I am learning in the process is that to be a "holy fool" is to live with such disregard for what others think of me that the love, truth, and grace of Christ is not obscured by living by the expectations of the world. To be a "holy fool" for Jesus' sake may mean that I befriend someone who is seen as a disadvantage; that I participate in an urban church that isn't comfortable, that I sit down next a homeless beggar for a chat, or that I donate to a "lost" cause. What might it mean for you to be a fool for Jesus' sake?

"... we have been made a spectacle to the whole universe, to angels as well as to men. We are fools for Christ! ... we go hungry and thirsty, we are in rags, we are brutally treated, we are homeless. We work hard with our own hands. When we are cursed, we bless; when we are persecuted, we endure it; when we are slandered, we answer kindly. Up to this moment we have become the scum of the earth, the refuse of the world" (1 Cor. 4:9-13).

CHAPTER 22

BRINGING HOPE TO LIFE

Martin Luther King was undoubtedly one of the most courageous prophets of the last century, and is widely recognized as the courageous leader who championed the cause of racial justice and equality in America. His passion for social justice has become immortalized in the words of a rousing speech he delivered on the steps of the Lincoln Memorial in 1963, just one hundred years after Abraham Lincoln abolished slavery in 1863. Despite the abolition of slavery, African Americans had continued to suffer the consequences of racism and discrimination in every aspect of their lives. Their hopes and dreams for racial equality had not been achieved simply by the proclamation of emancipation.

One hundred years later, as the civil rights movement was gaining momentum, Martin Luther King dared to give public voice to the unrealized dream of his anguished people,

> *"I have a dream that one day this nation will rise up and live out the true meaning of its creed: **'We hold these truths to be self-evident, that all men are created equal'** ... I have a dream that one day on the red hills of Georgia the sons of former slaves and the sons of former slave owners will be able to sit down together at the table of brotherhood.*

> *I have a dream that my four little children will one day live in a nation where they will not be judged by the color of their skin but by the content of their character."*

King not only dreamed the dream but gave himself to the cause by speaking up for justice and human dignity so that his children and his people could someday realize the dream of equality and dignity. Although best remembered for the legacy of his life and leadership in the American civil rights movement, his vision for justice encompassed all people who suffered the tyranny of social oppression and economic exploitation. In another speech delivered several months before his assassination, he observed:

> *"The developed industrial nations of the world cannot remain secure islands of prosperity in a seething sea of poverty. The storm is rising against the privileged minority of the earth, from which there is no shelter in isolation and armament. The storm will not abate until a just distribution of the fruits of the earth enables men everywhere to live in dignity and human decency."* [1]

The continuing exploitation of the poor and the weak is evidenced in societies throughout the world. The reality of this is seen in the gap between the powerful and the powerless; between the satisfied and the hungry; between the secure and the marginalized; between the wealthy and the destitute is an ever-widening chasm with countless people suffering in our own communities and around the world.

---

1 Martin Luther King Jr. *The Trumpet of Conscience* (Harper Collins, New York; 1968).

For millions of people are hopeless, voiceless, and powerless. But there are those who, like Martin Luther King, bring hope to life for those whose dreams are distant and diminished. These are people like you and me who work to

secure the rights and dignity of minority and marginalized
    people, resettle refugees from war and disaster,
liberate children from exploitation and slavery,
gain freedom of religion for those who are persecuted,
reconcile victims and offenders,
make peace in the face of war and conflict,
bring respect and care to the mentally challenged,
provide opportunity for the suffering poor,
comfort the dying.

These prophetic men and women not only dream of dignity for all people but enliven the dream as servants of God. Some would call them extremists, championing the cause of love and justice for all.

"Just as the eighth century prophets left their little villages and carried their 'thus saith the Lord' far beyond the boundaries of their home towns; and just as the Apostle Paul left his little village of Tarsus and carried the gospel of Jesus Christ to practically every hamlet and city of the Graeco-Roman world, I too am compelled to carry the gospel of freedom beyond my particular home town. Like Paul, I must constantly respond to the Macedonian call for aid ... I'm grateful to God that, through the Negro church, the dimension of non-violence entered our struggle. Was not Jesus an extremist for love. 'Love your enemies, bless them

that curse you, pray for them that despitefully use you.' Was not Amos an extremist for justice. 'Let justice roll down like waters and righteousness like a mighty stream.' Was not Paul an extremist for the gospel of Jesus Christ. 'I bear in my body the marks of the Lord Jesus.' Was not Martin Luther an extremist. 'Here I stand; I can do none other so help me God.' Was not John Bunyan an extremist. 'I will stay in jail to the end of my days before I make a butchery of my conscience.' ... So the question is not whether we will be extremist but what kind of extremist will we be. Will we be extremists for hate or will we be extremists for love? Will we be extremists for the preservation of injustice or will we be extremists for the cause of justice? In that dramatic scene on Calvary's hill, three men were crucified. We must not forget that all three were crucified for the same crime, the crime of extremism. Two were extremists for immorality, and thusly fell below their environment. The other, Jesus Christ, was an extremist for love, truth and goodness, and thereby rose above his environment.

There was a time when the church was very powerful. It was during that period when the early Christians rejoiced when they were deemed worthy to suffer for what they believed. In those days the church was not merely a thermometer that recorded the ideas and principles of popular opinion; it was a thermostat that transformed the mores of society. Whenever the early Christians entered a town the power structure got disturbed and immediately sought to convict them for being 'disturbers of the peace' and 'outside agitators.' But they went on with the conviction that they were 'a colony of heaven,' and had to obey God rather than man. They were small in number but big in commitment. They were too God-intoxicated to be 'astronomically intimidated.' They brought an end to such ancient evils as infanticide and gladiatorial contest." [2]

2   Martin Luther King Jr. Excerpts from his *Letter from a Birmingham Jail—16 April 1963.*

CHAPTER 23

MERCY IN THE JOURNEY

A friend challenged me to do something worthwhile with my life, to work with troubled kids, street children, and kids in conflict with the law. It was a challenge that would require me to leave the comfort and security of a small town, to leave a job with a future, and relocate to a very large and unfamiliar city without any job security at all. As irrational as it seemed, I knew that the cause was more important than my job. It was the beginning of a compelling and life-changing journey that has taken me into unfamiliar and fearful places, away from self-reliance and self-satisfaction; a merciful journey of learning to know myself and, more significantly, to know Jesus Christ.

Most of the juvenile offenders I worked with in the city were from broken homes and wasted their time on the streets in bad company. I worked hard building trust and friendship with them, engaging them in positive recreational and social activities. Initially I thought that my influence would make a visible difference in their lives. However, it didn't take long for me to realize that my investment of time and effort was bearing little fruit outside of the few hours I was able to spend with them each week.

Their values, habits, and behavior patterns were already so entrenched that even the positive influence of my spending five or six hours a week with them seemed short-lived. Although they were receptive and responsive during our time together, they would inevitably revert to the ways of the street. Many persisted in troublesome behavior at school and in the community, often ending up in police custody and juvenile court.

During the years I worked with those boys, the one thing that did seem to make a difference involved extended periods of time on wilderness camping experiences. Periodically I would take a small group of boys along with several counselors on canoe trips of a week or more. Taking only the barest of necessities, we paddled into remote wilderness areas far away from the distractions and attractions of the city streets. Inevitably, the first few days were extremely difficult, punctuated with expressions of fear and anger as the boys found themselves without recourse to the things that they were familiar with, their security. The boys struggled with the darkness, the stillness, and the unknown in an environment that was very different from the bustling city. Usually a couple of them would try to run away but they had no idea of direction in the woods. Others sulked and became angry when they realized that there was no way back and that the journey could only be completed through cooperation. Still others became loud and destructive only to realize that broken canoe paddles and torn tents only added to the difficulty and discomfort of their journey.

Yet these painful experiences eventually served to bring out the good in even the toughest guys. It didn't take many days for most of them to realize that each one had unique abilities and something to contribute to the group; that their survival depended on cooperation, not competition; that interdependence was more productive than independence or dependence; that there was a beautiful world beyond the familiar streets of the city. In the solitude of the wilderness, away from the clamor of their normal lives, the boys gradually began listening to each other, sharing more honestly, and exploring their personal fears, hurts, and needs.

For many of the guys these excursions down a wilderness river through unfamiliar forests initiated a journey into mercy, sensing God's presence and love and purpose for them. It was an experience that broke through their customary behavior patterns and stimulated personal growth at a deeper level. These wilderness trips became a starting point for change.

Journeys like that are not just for juvenile offenders and city kids. The journey from self-satisfaction and self-reliance to vulnerability, trust, and cooperation is our own journey as we learn to trust God in the unfamiliar wilderness of risking ourselves for the sake of others. The journey is both an outward journey of courage and compassion, and an inward journey of faith and dependence on the Lord.

The experience of putting ourselves on the line and risking ourselves for the sake of others is like a journey into the wilderness where we are invited to leave our familiar dependencies and face the silence, solitude, and deprivation that lies beyond the attractions and distractions that normally preoccupy our lives, even our spiritual lives. For me, it is often a journey in which God seems more poignantly real and present to me among the needy and broken people of the world than among my fellow congregants on most Sunday mornings.

As we distance ourselves from the familiar routines of pursuing our own interests, our lives become reshaped by a profound new sense of God's amazing grace for all people; and His power to transform our small acts of love in bringing hope and life and light into the dark recesses of human need.

THE VOYAGE [1]

The Children of Israel, God taking them,
Through the Red Sea obtained a path,
They obtained the quenching of their thirst
From a rock that might not by craftsman be hewn.

Who are they on the tiller of my rudder,
Giving speed to my east bound barge?
Peter and Paul and John the beloved,
Three to whom laud and [honor] are due
Who are the group near to my helm?
Peter and Paul and John the Baptist;
Christ is sitting on my helm,
Making guidance to the wind from the south.

To whom does tremble the voice of the wind?
To whom become tranquil strait and ocean?
To Jesus Christ, Chief of each saint,
Son of Mary, Root of victory,
Son of Mary, Root of victory.

---

1   Carmina Gadelica (Alexander Carmichael; Lindisfarne Press, NY, 1992 -- #120 p. 122).

CHAPTER 24

RESURRECTION AND THE
ROLLING STONES

One Holy Week on a Mexican prison island I experienced Easter. Fifty-five university students had chosen to spend their week-long Easter holiday on an island prison far removed from the comforts of home and all the enjoyment of a much-anticipated break from the tedium of studies and examinations. Along with two others, I had the privilege of accompanying the students on a special Policia Nacionale flight from Mexico City to a brown and barren island located nearly seventy miles offshore in the Pacific Ocean. Islas Marias has been a prison island since 1905 and is uninhabited except by prisoners, families of prisoners, corrections officials, and a cadre of marines.

As we stepped from the plane on to the tarmac at the end of a very short landing strip, we were met by the prison director, who showed us around the small island and recounted the story of his own spiritual transformation. His passion was to see Islas Marias become a centre for the spiritual and social transformation of prisoners and their families. "It is the only hope we have to overcome criminality," he stated matter-of-factly as he talked about his vision for the week-long student mission.

My colleagues from Prison Fellowship, the rector, and students from the University of Anahuac [1] all shared his buoyant hope and vision for the transformation of society. I noted the relevance of the university's motto *"Vince in Bono Malum"* (Good Overcomes all Evil) and its mission to "form positive leaders as agents of transformation, and to evangelize the culture by impregnating society with Christian values and ideas." Again and again these themes were reflected in the conversations I had with individual students. They spoke openly of their own spiritual journeys and their commitment to making a difference in the world by sharing the life, love, and light of Jesus Christ with others.

The substance of their passion was borne out in the fact that they were devoting the entire Easter holiday to living in very spartan conditions among prisoners and their families. "We don't come to change the lives of prisoners, we come as friends to show compassion and love, that's all. People open up and things happen," said one student. "I know that this experience will change me," said another, "because I believe Jesus is here and He changes people."

Looking into the eyes of the students at the beginning of Holy Week, the reflected light and hope of Jesus' resurrection was visible. The reality of the resurrection is evidenced and relived in the transformed lives of those who do good in the face of apathy, adversity, and evil. "Keep following Jesus, as the disciples followed Jesus to the tomb

1 The Universidad Anahuac México Sur is located in Olivar de los Padres, near Mexico City, and was established in 1979 by the Legionnaires of Christ.

of his friend Lazarus," I challenged the students before I left. "Jesus is always a friend to prisoners, and if you are a friend of Jesus then you also will be a friend to prisoners. Jesus loves them and wants to give them life and hope and freedom. This is something that you cannot do for them. But what you can do is what the friends of Jesus did at the tomb of Lazarus."

Jesus did not ask his friends to resuscitate Lazarus. He only asked them to roll the stone away from the entrance of the tomb and that is what they did. When they moved the stone, Jesus spoke into the darkness and the stench of the tomb, calling Lazarus back to life. Jesus is the one who gave life to Lazarus. You and I can't give life to anyone; we can't change their lives, only Jesus does that. What you and I can do, what Jesus asks us to do, is to roll the stones away. We are asked to move the obstacles that keep people from seeing and experiencing love, hope, and light. We do that by offering friendship and creating space in which the life-giving presence and words of Jesus can be heard. We do this because we are Easter people, friends of the Resurrected Jesus, the life-giver who alone can change the hearts and lives of prisoners.

As followers of Jesus, you and I are "rollers of the stones" in the continuing resurrection story.

"The resurrection faith is not proved true by means of historical evidence, or only in the next world. It is proved here and now, through the courage for revolt, the protest against deadly powers, and the self-giving of men and women for the victory of life. It is impossible to talk convincingly about

Christ's resurrection without participating in the movement of the Spirit 'who descends on all flesh' to quicken it. This movement of the Spirit is the divine 'liberation movement' for it is the process whereby the world is recreated. So resurrection means rebirth out of impotence and indolence to the 'living hope.' And today 'living hope' means a passion for life, and a lived protest against death." [2]

---

2   Jurgen Moltmann as quoted in *Bread and Wine: Readings for Lent and Easter* (Plough Publishing, Farmington, PA, USA; 2003 pp. 368-9).

Part D

Holy Subversion: Doing Justice, Loving Mercy, Walking Humbly

———◆———

CHAPTER 25

CONSEQUENCES UNDESERVED

Most of us simply assume that justice is done when offenders "get what they deserve," or when, in some way, they reap the consequences of their wrongdoing.

Well, I was about to get what I deserved. I knew I had it coming as the oncoming police cruiser, lights flashing, made a quick turn behind me as I sped by. After enduring a long day of frustrating delays and cancelled flights, it was very late and I was anxious to get home from the airport. I was in a hurry, trying to make up for lost time.

"Do you know why I pulled you over?" asked the police officer. "Yes," I responded, "I guess I was going a bit too fast."

"Do you know how fast you were going?"

"No, I have no idea at all. I just want to get home. I'm a day late because of airport problems and cancelled flights."

"Ninety seven," said the officer sternly. "That's awfully fast for this road. You do know the posted speed limit is seventy."

"I understand. No excuses; I just wasn't paying attention."

"Have you been pulled over for speeding before?" he asked.

"No, I haven't," I responded, while acknowledging in the privacy of my mind that I am actually a frequent but careful speeder. As the police officer returned to his patrol car, I resigned myself to the fact that I was about to reap the overdue consequences of my habitual tendency to drive above the posted speed limit. It seemed like a long wait on the side of the road, a wait made conspicuously longer by passing motorists who slowed as they passed in order to see if they could recognize the offending speeder. I felt embarrassed as car after car drove by, and I recognized several of them as cars I had hastily overtaken along the way. I could almost hear the occupants of those cars nodding agreement and saying, "Now, that's what I call justice!" I could hear them because I've so often said the same thing when passing other hapless speeders.

When the officer finally came back, he handed over my driving license and vehicle papers. "Have a good day, Mr Nikkel, and please watch your speed from now on. You don't want to be a fatality on your way home."

That was it, there was no deserved speeding ticket, no penalty to pay! What luck! What mercy! I'm not sure if justice was served or not, but in not getting what I knew I deserved I got what I did not deserve. The grace that the officer extended made a far greater impression on me than if I had received the penalty I deserved for my violation of the law.

John's Gospel recounts the story of Jesus' encounter with a beggar who had been blind since birth. Eager to make sense of the situation, the disciples asked Jesus, "Who sinned, this man or his parents, that he was born blind?" Is his condition the consequence of his own fault or that of his parents? Is his blindness deserved? Many times I have heard the very same question asked about people who are homeless, have AIDS, or are imprisoned. Inevitably, the question implies that the person is to blame, for the fault lines often seem to be so clear.

There is a cause-and-consequence logic in assessing responsibility and blame, in seeking justice. In Jesus' day it was commonly held that physical imperfections were the consequence of sin, God's justice. But Jesus pointedly said that it is not about finding fault. Rather, the blindness in this case was an occasion for the grace and mercy of God to be made visible. Jesus was not concerned with tracing fault lines (John 9:1-34).

No human being, whatever their life condition, should be seen simplistically as being at fault, as getting what they deserve. Whatever their condition might be, by whatever cause, it is an opportunity for us to show God's grace and mercy. Whether at fault or not, contributing to their own suffering or not, whenever and wherever people find themselves in any kind of turmoil or in any kind of trouble, "We must do the works of him who sent [Jesus]."

It is our human tendency to demand punishment and consequences from judgment and justice. It is so logical, so matter-of-fact, to give people the penalty that their behavior deserves. But God's justice is not the justice of giving people the penalties they deserve. God's justice is tempered with mercy, giving us what we don't deserve. Love and justice meet on the cross where God takes upon Himself the consequences of our offences so that we can be free. Jesus, the innocent one, suffering on the cross undermines our notions of what justice is all about.

> *Jesus*
> *the excluded one*
> *is close to a blind*
> *and excluded beggar.*
> *Jesus heals him.*
> *Some of the Pharisees are blind to the miracle.*
> *We too can be blinded*
> *by an ideology* [1]

---

1   Jean Vanier *(Drawn into the Mystery of Jesus through the Gospel of John,* Novalis, Ottawa; 2004) p. 169.

CHAPTER 26

ULTIMATE JUSTICE

"He now faces a sentence imposed by a higher power ... It is terminal, final and irrevocable. He is going to die." [1]

Is it true that final justice is ultimately and irrevocably imposed by death's "Grim Reaper"? Why are people inclined to take satisfaction in, or often even gloat over, justice being served when a "bad" person is about to die or be put to death, while at the same time they grieve the injustice and unfairness of death prematurely taking the life of a "good" person?

In a rather controversial decision, the Scottish government granted early release to Abdelbaset al-Megrahi, who had been convicted and imprisoned for the 1988 bombing of Pan American Flight 103 over Lockerbie, Scotland. After serving just over eight years of a twenty-seven year sentence, al-Megrahi, who was suffering from terminal cancer, was granted early release on compassionate grounds. "Our

---

1 Scottish Justice Secretary Kenny MacAskill, quoted on the release from prison of Abdelbaset al-Megrahi, who had been convicted in the 1988 bombing of Pan Am Flight 103 over Lockerbie, Scotland, in which 270 people were killed. (*Los Angeles Times* news report by Henry Chu, reporting from London, August 21, 2009). http://www.latimes.com/news/nationworld/world/la-fg-lockerbie-release21-2009aug21,0,220813.story

beliefs dictate that justice be served but mercy be shown,"[2] said Justice Secretary Kenny MacAskill, who went on to suggest that, in spite of such mercy, justice will still be ultimately served because al-Megrahi will die.

As I followed the ensuing heated political debate and the public responses of the family members of the Pan Am victims to news of al-Megrahi's release, it seemed to me that nobody was satisfied with either justice or with mercy. There were those who felt that justice was being undermined by compassion. On the other side were those who felt that human compassion was rendered meaningless by those who invoked death as the final arbiter of justice.

Surely if human beings have some capacity to be compassionate and merciful, then God our Creator is even more perfectly compassionate and merciful. And surely the demands of justice are not satisfied by death, for we all die—offenders and victims alike. In a real sense, justice can never be satisfied just through punishment alone but through repentance and forgiveness; through healing and restoration by God's grace. St Augustine observed that justice without mercy is but tyranny and that mercy without justice is weakness; but that justice and mercy meet in the grace of God alone.

I have corresponded and met with men who were convicted and sentenced to death by the demands of justice. I have been deeply moved by those among them who faced the gallows, electric chair, or firing squad as the final decree of justice, believing that they would be embraced by the

---

2 ibid.

ultimate mercy of God. Fr Brian Massie and Rev. Henry Khoo served as prison chaplains in Jamaica and Singapore respectively. For years both men walked in the painful company of prisoners on death row during their final hours. Some of those prisoners had come to embrace forgiveness through Jesus Christ and literally found themselves clinging to life between ultimate human justice and ultimate divine mercy. Squeezed between the merciless justice of the gallows and the embracing grace of Jesus Christ that triumphs over human justice—they clung to hope.

I often grieve for the victims of injustice and I am incensed by those who perpetrate evil and cause untold suffering. I grieve for the men, women, and children who lost their lives in the bombing over Lockerbie. Every one of them died prematurely at the hands of inhumanity and evil. I hurt for their surviving friends and families, who have suffered a loss that can never be repaired or repaid, regardless of whether al-Megrahi had been held in prison until he died or simply died in freedom. I have prayed for the victims, as I have also prayed for offenders like al-Megrahi.

Only mercy can heal the damage of injustice and truly satisfy the demands of justice. Justice is not satisfied only in punishing offenders, but in healing the damage done by crime, in repairing relationships that have been violated and in restoring the peace of the community. I pray for myself and for those of us who are trying to come to terms with mercy and the demands of justice, that we might yet learn to act justly and to love mercy and to live in humility (Micah 6:8) before the One in whom justice and mercy ultimately meet.

To seek justice with mercy is to break the unending cycle of crime and violence. Violence that is countered only with violent and punitive justice will never result in peace.

CHAPTER 27

A TRUE CONFESSION

If ever there was a scoundrel who deserved harsh consequences it was probably Bernard Madoff , the unscrupulous investment manager from New York. He was accused of stealing nearly $50 billion worth of investments from his clients. His victims, many of them elderly investors, came forward telling heartbreaking stories of losing their entire life's savings, or their retirement funds, to his manipulative schemes. They were people who trusted Madoff as a friend and financial advisor, but he deliberately betrayed their trust. Yet Mr Madoff neither admitted his guilt nor directly apologized to any of his victims. And why would he, for in doing so he would be taking personal responsibility for their pain. How much easier it is to plead guilty to the prosecutor than to look one's victims in the eyes.

Bernard Madoff is not the only person who prefers to face the prosecutor instead of his victims for the prosecutor is an impartial bystander. There are both legal as well as personal consequences to most crimes, and offenders usually find it far easier to deal with the legal rather than with the painful personal consequences.

There is a sense in which I am no different from Bernard Madoff when I confess my sins and transgressions to Almighty God without ever directly facing the persons I have offended or hurt. I approach God as if He is an impartial prosecutor or judge who has not been personally hurt by the things I've done. *"Nothing against you Lord, it's just a human being I've had some trouble with."* So I tell God the truth of what I've done, asking for His mercy and forgiveness, and then I get up to get on with my life. How frequently I do this, simply because it is so much easier than having to face real people, my victims, who painfully remember how I hurt them.

In reflecting on the story of Bernard Madoff, and in realizing my own tendency to avoid admitting responsibility to the victims of my offenses, I recognize anew that Jesus also knows the victim and cares for the victim, and He takes my offense and my sins personally. He takes my gossip, lust, greed, anger, disrespect, lies, selfishness, racism, judgmental and unforgiving attitude, arrogance and insensitivity, and any other act by which I offend another person personally. Jesus is as much my victim as the person I offend or sin against, for He is neither impervious nor impartial to the things I do and say that denigrate and damage people.

A true confession is admitting my guilt and taking personal responsibility for my actions before God and before my victims. There is no place for hiding behind legalities and rationalizations in order to avoid looking my victims in the eye and humbly saying, "I'm sorry. Please forgive me."

Jesus said ...

"Therefore, if you are offering your gift at the altar
and there remember that your brother has
something against you,
leave the gift there in front of the altar.
First go and be reconciled to your brother;
then come and offer your gift." (Matt. 5:23-24)

CHAPTER 28

PLAYING WITH FIRE

He was ten years old and probably should have known better than to play with fire. But most kids that age tend to be more focused on the gratification of the moment than on the possibility of unintended consequences. Whether it was simply curiosity, or a fascination with fire, that led him to play with matches that day is not clear, but the magnitude of destruction resulting from a small fire that turned into a raging wild fire sweeping across thousands of acres in California was devastating.[1]

We've all had close encounters with the unanticipated trajectory of a careless word or action going far beyond anything we ever intended. As a teenager I remember firing a loaded shotgun from the window of a speeding truck. It was a simple dare on a Sunday afternoon; the fence posts along a country road were my target. With two shots fired and one to go, I didn't notice the farmhouse until it was too late. Suddenly I came face to face with a scenario that took the fun right out of what I was doing. Fortunately, no one was hurt and no damage was done, but my resulting encounter with the police made me realize just how

---

1 *As reported in World News by Charles Gibson -- ABC News Law & Justice Unit. Nov. 2, 2007.*

serious the unintended consequences of my careless and impulsive actions could have been.

Just as it didn't cross my mind that those fence post shots might come close to injuring or even killing someone, I am sure that the ten-year-old boy didn't think his playing with matches would eventually culminate in 38,000 acres being burned, 21 homes being destroyed, and more than 15,000 people forced to flee the raging fire. Playing with fire had unintended consequences!

Responsible parents try to teach kids about these things. But in one way or another, kids throughout the ages have always tested those parental warnings to see for themselves if the stove is really as hot as their parents have told them. Even as adults we are prone to play with fire. The world's prisons echo with stories of men and women who had neither intention nor any inkling that their actions would result in imprisonment. The inferno that is prison is not what they had in mind when they began playing with fire.

Of course, some people are aware of the risks of playing with fire, but they don't take those risks seriously. It is only when something goes unexpectedly awry that they awaken to the reality and the magnitude of unintended consequences that are way beyond their ability to contain or control. But there are those of us who think there is no risk at all, and that the things we play with are not really as dangerous as playing with fire. And so in the hidden places of our hearts and minds we harbor envy, lust, falsehood, manipulation, consumption, and revenge. There seems to be no risk, no exposure in playing with these matches, until something is ignited that we can't control.

The real problem in playing with matches is not just about consequences or the magnitude of those consequences. The real wrongdoing is playing with matches, the action itself, seen or unseen. It is so easy for us to point our fingers at those whose guilt screams from the headlines or those whose actions have inescapable consequences. But the justice we demand is the justice we also deserve, for we are all offenders and our guilt is as much for our intentions as for the unintended consequences, like the boy who played with fire.

There but for the grace of God ...

CHAPTER 29

NO HONOR AMONG THIEVES

There is no honor among thieves. It is often observed that human greed is more powerful than human loyalty and that no allegiance or promise is safe from corruption by money, sex, or power. Stories of double-crossing, double-dealing, and betrayal are rife in the world of crime. Many of the most popular crime novels grip the reader with intrigue and it isn't possible to guess who did it until the very end. Surprise endings typically involve a character or characters who seemed trustworthy only to be found working for the other side.

Prisoners all over the world have told me stories of being betrayed by accomplices they thought were friends. Among those prison inmates who are most universally despised and victimized are informants who have double-crossed their friends or partners in crime for personal benefit, often betraying them to the police. On the other side, among the most respected prisoners are those who have refused to inform on their partners, taking the blame, and serving time in prison rather than implicating others.

Loyalty and betrayal are the currency of honor and respect in prison, just as in society. The only real problem for any of us comes when loyalty is for sale to the highest bidder. For the right price people can be induced to switch their citizenship, friendships, church affiliation, and life partners as easily as they switch their loyalty from one football team to another. For some the price is high, for others low, while for yet others the cost of loyalty is a price they don't want to pay.

A popular speaker and friend of mine told a story about a beautiful woman who found herself alone in a hotel lift with an equally attractive man. As the elevator slowly ascended to the twentieth floor of the hotel, the man looked at the woman approvingly and asked, "Would you be interested in coming to bed with me if I gave you a million dollars?" "Why, certainly I would," was her immediate response. A short silence followed as they both pondered the proposition. He broke the silence, "How about if I gave you $200,000, would you sleep with me for that?" "Yes," she responded, "I could do that." But he continued, "If I give you $50,000, would you still come with me?" "Sure," she replied, albeit somewhat hesitantly and without enthusiasm. "And if you don't mind me asking just one more time. Would you sleep with me for just $100?" Shocked and indignant, the woman slapped his face, "Absolutely not!" she screamed. "Just what kind of a person do you take me for?" "Lady," the man responded, "we already established what kind of person you are. It was just the price we were discussing."

While the story is perhaps apocryphal, the point it makes is uncomfortably clear. For it isn't just the story of a woman and man in an elevator, it is a story that touches on our human nature and the price we put on loyalty and morality. How often do we sell ourselves to the highest bidder, when the price is right? It isn't always in the big things of life but in the little things too. When I schedule time to meet a friend and something more interesting comes up, what do I do? All too often I find some lame excuse to back out of the prior commitment in order to take on a new one that is more appealing and attractive. In friendships, business dealings, and my everyday lesser and greater commitments, by what measure do I stay the course? Is it by loyalty and honor or is it by the measure of what's in it for me?

The story of Judas is very interesting. He was a follower of Jesus, one of His closest disciples who knew Jesus as a companion and teacher. He had witnessed the blind receiving sight, lepers healed, beggars transformed, and even the dead being raised to life. Judas knew the gospel. How could he not know the message of Jesus inside out? And yet he sold his loyalty and his honor, betraying Jesus for personal gain and possibly to save himself. It is said of Judas that he was a thief, helping himself to funds in the common purse. The roots of his betrayal began in little things, and being loyal only to himself he betrayed the man who was his friend.

If you cannot trust your friends—can they trust you?

> *This world's a jungle there ain't no justice*
> *Laws of nature rule this land.*
> *Better hide your horses, bury your whiskey*
> *Hold your woman any way you can*

Cause there ain't no right or wrong, nothing's
   carved in stone
   It ain't cheating if you don't get caught
Jokers laugh and losers grieve
   Cause out here there's no honor among thieves. [1]

---

1 From a country and western song *"No Honor Among Thieves"* by Toby Keith.

CHAPTER 30

BY ANY OTHER NAME

"What's in a name?
That which we call a rose, by any other name would smell as sweet;
so Romeo would, were he not Romeo call'd,
retain that dear perfection which he owes without that title."
(William Shakespeare, *Romeo and Juliet*)

"So what is your impression of our institution?" asked the Minister of Justice. "Did you notice any changes?"

I knew it was a loaded question and, for a moment, I wished that it was possible for me to avoid responding. Everyone's eyes were on me. We had just toured the main correctional facility of his country's renamed prison system, and I had been very impressed by the physical conditions, cleanliness, and extensive education and job training programs. There was indeed much that I found commendable in his institution as compared to the terrible overcrowding, crumbling infrastructure, reeking sanitation, and pervasive idleness that characterize many of the other prison systems in Africa.

But that was not what the Minister of Justice was asking. He wanted to know if I saw any substantive differences in the prisons following the name change of the prison system to "Correctional Services," in keeping with a growing international trend to change the nature of, and attitude toward, imprisonment, especially among prison officers.

"To be honest," I responded, "I did not see any substantive change. In fact, what I noticed was a system that seems to be very militaristic." Seldom, outside of the military services, had I seen such consciousness of rank and overt displays of authority, from the uniforms to the barking of commands and the snappy salutes. Clearly, even the lowest-ranking "correctional" officer was far above the status of inmates who were without rank or power or significance. Correctional services or not, the prisoners were still being treated as prisoners in every sense of the name, and the relational climate between officers and inmates was anything but dignifying.

During my university years I had a very close friend who was so decidedly unhappy with his names that he had them legally changed. However, changing his names didn't change his personality, and certainly had no bearing on the quality of our relationship, nor did it affect how he was perceived by others. As is so frequently the case, although names are important, merely changing a name or a label is not efficacious in changing the content or the essence of something. Changing the name of a prison to "correctional center" does not make it any less a prison or any more corrective. A prison is still a prison, regardless of what it is called. No amount of renaming can improve the attitudes of guards toward inmates, elevate the experience of being incarcerated, or remove the pain of being helpless and separated from one's family.

Whatever a prison may be called, those who are incarcerated are rehabilitated not by change of name or program, or even by improvement of conditions, but by an inner change through the love and mercy of Jesus Christ. In the chapel of the prison (correctional institution) I met a young man who had been condemned to death. With just days to go before his execution, he was recommended for pardon because of the radical change evidenced in his attitude and behavior. Yet his name was still the same as it was when he was facing execution. The change in his life was not a change in name but a change in heart, and he told me that God has called him to be a pastor not a prisoner, to preach the good news to others!

It takes a fundamental change in perspective and values to reform the essential character of a prison system or of a person. A prison becomes truly correctional only when it becomes a place where offenders are treated with dignity and respect, and where they can find help and healing. Until that happens, by any other name a prison is still a prison.

There is no human institution, rehabilitation program or social therapy that can transform the character of an offender. Only the transforming love and grace of God can do that. This is a reality that I see most powerfully in the prisons of the world and it is a truth that undermines the powers of the world. This is the subversive message that we who follow Jesus live out as we proclaim and demonstrate the transforming, life-changing love of God through our relationships, our work, and our lives.

CHAPTER 31

FALL FROM GRACE

There was no way of avoiding, denying, or covering up the successive revelations of his marital infidelities. One by one, sordid accounts of his sexual trysts with other women caught the attention of the media and the public. Overnight, the squeaky-clean image as a self-controlled professional, and wholesome and inspiring role model to a needy generation of young men became undone. Disappointed, embarrassed, hurt, and even angered by his betrayal of their trust, many of his supporters, friends, and even family abandoned him. Tiger Woods, one of the most famous and successful golfers of all time, had fallen from grace. Tiger's story is by no means unique, and would hardly make the news but for the fact that the public had held him in high esteem. He was a disappointing celebrity. Almost every day brings news of those whose appearance of decency becomes undone by their uninhibited appetite and passions.

Like Tiger Woods, many of those who fall try everything they can to make a comeback, starting afresh in order to earn back a place of favor. Sometimes they are able to work their way back. But there is one thing I've learned among men and women in prison who feel that they have fallen so low that they are in a place where they have to look up to see bottom. It is this: when a person has fallen so low that there is no way back for him, he has actually fallen into a place of grace.

Regardless of how low a person might have fallen, they have not fallen from grace but have literally fallen into grace. When a person is reduced to helplessness, the only hope is unmerited grace. It is a gift. It is a place where celebrities and criminals, you and I can only realize and accept that our dependence is not on the fleeting tide of public favor, but on God's grace alone.

There is a poignant anecdote about a young soldier who served as a sentry under Napoleon during the war between France and England. In the heat of battle he threw down his weapon and deserted his post, only to be captured, tried, and subsequently sentenced to death. His widowed mother, devastated by the prospect of losing her only son, appealed directly to Napoleon for mercy on his behalf. "Mercy!" spat Napoleon. "Your son is not deserving of mercy." "Yes, I know, he does not deserve mercy," she responded. "But that is exactly why he needs it."

Like mercy, grace is not about getting what any of us deserve; it is getting what we do not deserve. Grace is not a commodity that rises and falls like the stock market; it is the constant of God's love. Grace cannot be gained by hard work or good behavior; it is only something we can receive or turn away from. Grace is not something we fall out of, but inevitably it is something we fall into. When you and I face our greatest embarrassment or failure, when we completely lose face before our friends and family and even ourselves, only grace can lift and heal us. Grace is Jesus Christ, God incarnate, stooping down to embrace sinful and stubborn human beings in our places of failure and need.

> *A crucial eccentricity of the Christian faith is the assertion that people are saved by grace. It is almost as though God says, Here is your life. You might never have been, but you are because the party wouldn't have been complete without you. Here is the world. Beautiful and terrible things will happen. Don't be afraid; I am with you. Nothing can ever separate us. It's for you I created the universe. I love you. There's only one catch. Like any other gift, the gift of grace can be yours only if you'll reach out and take it. Maybe being able to reach out and take it is a gift too.[1]*

---

1   Frederick Buechner, *Wishful Thinking, a Theological ABC* (William Collins & Sons, London, 1973) p. 34.

CHAPTER 32

PARDON AND ACCEPTANCE

"What do you think of forgiveness?" a friend once asked me. Without waiting for a response, she declared that, as far as she was concerned, forgiveness is completely irresponsible. "They will just do it again," she said. "Forgiveness lets people off the hook and they don't have to take responsibility for their actions."

I don't know if there was a particular incident or situation that she was reacting to, although the community where she lives has been plagued with hooliganism, and the residents have been able to do very little about it.

"What if someone asks to be forgiven?" I responded. "Do they then deserve forgiveness?"

"Well, yes, maybe. But that is completely different," she replied.

"And what if someone who has been convicted of a crime is released from prison after serving his sentence. He has done his time. Should he not be forgiven?"

"It depends if he deserves it or not."

"And what does it take for someone to deserve forgiveness?" I asked. "And how long should we hold someone's crime against him? Isn't forgiveness also about releasing ourselves from carrying a burden of anger and revenge?"

I wish I could say that our conversation ended on a positive note, but it didn't. We agreed to disagree and changed the subject. The intensity of that discussion about forgiveness is not uncommon. Sometimes it is also a public debate, as was the case following the release of two high-profile prisoners. Chris Rwakasisi, the former Minister of Security in Uganda, was granted a presidential pardon after serving twenty-four years in prison under sentence of death. Tamrat Layne, the former Prime Minister of Ethiopia, was granted amnesty and released after serving twelve years in prison.

While I was filled with joy and gratitude at the release of these two men, whom I know and who have been touched by Prison Fellowship, their release from prison was not greeted with enthusiasm by everyone. There were those who thought that neither man had yet paid his debt to society.

Shortly after his release, Tamrat Layne appeared in a church where he told his moving story of finding hope and new life in Jesus Christ during imprisonment. "I have repented and I know that God has forgiven me," he said. "I will never be the same." The very day that Chris Rwakasisi was released he also went to church to pray and to praise God for His grace and mercy. "The Lord appeared to me in my lonely solitary cell when I felt like I was at the end of the rope," he told a reporter. "It was the turning point in my life." "When I sincerely asked for forgiveness, I believe that God forgave me." [1]

---

1   *Daily Monitor* article by Lulu Jemimah (January 24, 2009).

There is no question that both men, in spite of their notoriety and the lack of public grace, have been transformed by the grace and mercy of God. They have been forgiven, not because they deserved or earned it or repaid their debt to society, but because they accepted it. Forgiveness is not something a person can purchase; it can only be received.

In 1915 George Burdick, City Editor for *The New York Tribune*, appeared before a federal grand jury investigating allegations of fraud that he had documented in an investigative article. Burdick adamantly refused to testify and refused to reveal his sources. In the wake of a growing impasse, US President Woodrow Wilson granted Burdick "a full and unconditional pardon for all offenses against the United States" that he might have committed in connection with the article and for any other matter the grand jury might ask him about. Yet Burdick refused to accept the pardon and was subsequently locked up for contempt of court. In the ensuing, complicated legal battles, it was eventually determined that a pardon is an act of grace, the validity of which depends on its acceptance. It cannot be forced upon a person.

Forgiveness changes both the person who extends forgiveness and the one who accepts it. To reject pardon, human or divine, is to choose one's own spiritual, emotional, mental, and even physical imprisonment. To forgive someone is not to take that person off the hook of responsibility, but to offer that person a way forward, a way out of the cycle of guilt and anger.

Nothing worth doing is completed in our lifetime,
  Therefore, we are saved by hope.
Nothing true or beautiful or good makes complete sense
  in any immediate context of history;
  Therefore, we are saved by faith.
Nothing we do, however virtuous, can be accomplished
  alone.
  Therefore, we are saved by love.
No virtuous act is quite as virtuous from the standpoint
  of our friend or foe as from our own;
Therefore, we are saved by the final form of love which
  is forgiveness. (Reinhold Niebuhr)

CHAPTER 33

THE RE-ENACTMENT

I sat spellbound as a group of inmates performed a short drama in the prison chapel. Behind them were the chapel altar and a large crucifix depicting a bloodied, suffering Jesus hanging on the cross. The actors, female prisoners wearing costumes that they had made, performed their roles with passion and compelling eloquence. In the audience, some of the prisoners who had been watching began wiping tears from their eyes. I fought to hold back my own tears as the impact of the story they were re-enacting beside the altar and the crucifix washed over me. It was their story—captured in the story of a woman victimized, singled out, and humiliated.

Onstage, a group of the performers pointed accusatory fingers at the solitary figure of a woman crouching in fear. Their eyes stabbed at her with cold, menacing judgment, stripping her of every shred of decency and dignity. Shrill voices demanded justice, punishment for her sins. As the scene climaxed, an actor playing the role of Jesus unexpectedly departed from the script. Falling to the floor beside her fellow prisoner, she sobbed uncontrollably, wrapping her arms around the weeping, trembling woman who was being accused as if for real.

As the two of them wept together, the harsh voices of accusation and outrage gave way to an awesome, holy silence. The pointing fingers of the accusers that had seemed so menacing began to wipe the tears from their own eyes. They knew that this was no mere drama; it was real. It was the life experience of every one of them.

As I observed this emotional scene, my mind resonated with the unfinished lines of the story, of Jesus kneeling on the ground beside the woman in grace before her accusers "If any one of you is without sin, let him be the first to throw a stone! ...Woman, where are they? Has no-one condemned you? ... Then neither do I condemn you," Jesus declared (John 8:7-11).

The re-enactment by the female prisoners in the chapel of Santa Monica prison culminated on a bittersweet note. I realized the painful parallel between the lives of the women in that prison and the story of the woman caught, accused, and publicly humiliated by being mercilessly dragged by her accusers into the public square to be judged by Jesus. But Jesus did not judge her. His response was every bit as unexpected as the spontaneous response of the actor in the play. Rather than remaining at a distance from the woman being accused, Jesus embraced her with forgiveness and respect. It was the forgiveness and respect that every woman in Santa Monica prison was yearning for, crying out for, as the dramatic performance gave way to a deeper reality. It is the same kind of forgiveness that each one of us hungers for in the face of our own failures and sin.

As much as we try to keep our mistakes and faults hidden from public view, when we are exposed it isn't judgment we need but forgiveness, understanding, and respect. But in response to the faults and failings of others, we find it so very difficult to let them off the hook of accusation and judgment. We tend to stand at a distance pointing out their faults and demanding justice and punishment. Forgiveness in response to failure is an unnatural act that goes against every instinct we have of fair play. In the economies of human crime, punishment, and justice, forgiveness makes no logical or emotional sense, except when we ourselves need it. Then it's the only way of release from guilt and its consequence.

Forgiveness is an undeserved gift of freedom. The woman who was accused and brought to Jesus was forgiven and not condemned, just as the woman in the play had her dignity and life restored when accusations and judgment were replaced by love and grace. But the forgiveness that Jesus extended to that woman, and the forgiveness He extends to us, comes at a price. The accusers in the story may have thought that Jesus would share their indignation and mete out judgment, but He didn't. By extending forgiveness instead of judgment, Jesus ultimately sacrificed His life on behalf of sinners.

Three centuries ago, Alexander Pope immortalized the observation that "to err is human, to forgive, divine." [1] It is probably true, for sin and error and failure mar the lives of every human being. Like the inmates in Santa Monica

---

1 Alexander Pope in *"An Essay on Criticism,"* published in 1711.

prison, we often find ourselves in a place of guilt, yearning for pardon, release, and reinstatement. We err and long to be forgiven.

As I looked at the tear-stained faces of the prisoners around me, many of them young, I wondered who would come to re-enact the love and grace of Jesus in the dust of accusation and rejection in their lives, and embrace them with forgiveness. I am convinced that there is nothing more unnatural, yet more divine, than our daily re-enactment of Jesus' grace and love as we forgive.

> *Be kind and compassionate to one another, forgiving each other, just as in Christ God forgave you. Be imitators of God, therefore, as dearly loved children and live a life of love, just as Christ loved us and gave himself up for us as a fragrant offering and sacrifice to God* (Eph. 4:32–5:2).

Writing to the fourth century Church, St John Chrysostom said:

> *What are you saying? "Shall I forgive him?" Christ is saying, "Yes!" This sacrifice was instituted for the sake of peace with your brother. Accordingly, if the sacrifice was instituted for the sake of peace with your brother, but if you do not establish peace, you partake of the sacrifice in vain; the work has become of no profit to you. Do first, then, that for the sake of which the sacrifice is offered and then you will properly enjoy its benefits. The Son of God came down for this purpose, to reconcile our human nature to the Lord. But He did not come down for that purpose alone, but also for the purpose of making us, if we do likewise, sharers of His title. For He says: "Blessed are the peacemakers, for they shall*

be called sons of God" (Matt. 5:9). *You, according to your human capacity, must do what the only begotten Son of God has done, be an agent of peace, for yourself and for others. For this reason, at the very time of sacrifice He recalls to us no other commandment than that of reconciliation with one's brother, showing that it is the greatest of all.* [2]

---

2   St John Chrysostom.

Part E

The Way of Jesus: Bringing Hope to Life

CHAPTER 34

COLOR FOR LIFE

"You cannot imagine how exciting it is for us when you come to visit us in prison," declared the ex-prisoner. "You not only bring us help; you bring us color. All we see in prison is colorless and gray. There is not much color in prison and when you volunteers come in we see colors that are like life; they aren't the colors of prison."

I hadn't thought about my work being colorful before. I am a frequent traveler between two worlds: between free communities that nurture creativity and life, and prisons that enforce conformity and containment; between communities that sing with vibrant sounds and luster, and prisons that groan with monotony and dreariness. I commute between the openness of communities and the restricting walls of the prison world.

To describe the prison world as dull and drab is not an understatement. While visiting several African prisons, I saw again the dull, boring, and monochromatic world of imprisonment made even drearier by the crumbling infrastructures, poverty, idleness, and overcrowding about which that ex-prisoner had spoken. As much as in any other region of the world, most of Africa's prisons are devoid of liveliness and one can actually feel the life being sucked out of the inmates. In every respect, both imprisonment and the prison environment leach life and vitality out of human beings: physically, mentally, socially, and spiritually.

It has long been observed that the tragedy of imprisonment is not that it prevents normal contact and conversation between prisoners and their friends and family, but that it prevents the normal community from coming in, from having any influence. I haven't given this much thought except for the idea that the involvement of the community in prison serves as a necessary bridge between prisoners and their community. Since crime is a problem of the community, somehow the community must be part of the solution because eventually the vast majority of prisoners will be released back into the communities from which they came. In what condition will they leave prison?

After being separated from the vitality and life of the community, will they be able to successfully reintegrate? A bridge of social, material, and spiritual friendship is essential for prisoner re-entry. It isn't easy for men and women who have become blind to the colors of humanity to regain their sense of balance in being fully human and alive.

As I listened to the African ex-prisoner share his experience of imprisonment and his subsequent return to the community, I became poignantly aware of just how degrading and damaging imprisonment is and how life-affirming and revitalizing it is for inmates when volunteers come in to visit them. I've tended to think that the principal value of prison volunteers is in their messages of hope and faith and in their compassionate friendship. Quite possibly the color of their presence conveys the message of life and hope just as powerfully as their words.

"Color gives us feelings of life and joy," said the ex-prisoner. "I am glad you came to visit me; it gave me hope and kept me alive." His words echo the message of Paul to the followers of Jesus when he told them that they were "the aroma of Christ—the fragrance of life" (2 Cor. 2:15-16) in the world. His words also echo Jesus' poignant challenge to His followers not to be tasteless or hidden in the shadows but to be salt and light in the world (Matt. 5:13-14).

To inspire hope and life among people who feel hurt and cut off from life is as much about the color, fragrance, and flavor of our presence among people in difficulty as it is about our efforts to speak and to serve.

> *So many nights I'd sit by my window*
> *Waiting for someone to sing me his song*
> *So many dreams I kept deep inside me*
> *Alone in the dark but now*
> *You've come along*
> *You light up my life*
> *You give me hope*
> *To carry on*
> *You light up my days*
> *and fill my nights with song*
> *Rollin' at sea, adrift on the water*
> *Could it be finally I'm turning for home?*
> *Finally, a chance to say hey,*
> *I love You*
> *Never again to be all alone* [1]

---

1 Excerpts from *"You Light Up My Life,"* a country and western song composed by Joe Brooks.

CHAPTER 35

WAR AND PEACE

If there is light in the soul,
there will be beauty in the person.
If there is beauty in the person,
there will be harmony in the house.
If there is harmony in the house,
there will be order in the nation.
If there is order in the nation,
there will be peace in the world. [1]

Ironically, just days before he accepted the Nobel Peace Prize, US President Barack Obama announced a major increase in military deployment, a troop surge, in Afghanistan. It is just as ironic, I suppose, that the Peace Prize itself was established by Alfred Nobel, the inventor of dynamite and ballistite—two destructive explosives that have had huge military applications and caused untold destruction. [2] When it comes to the quest for peace, we find ourselves living in a world of irony. It is easier to talk about peace than to make peace and we blindly continue to believe that peace can be won through war and conflict!

---

1   Chinese Proverb.

2   http://www.britannica.com/EBchecked/topic/50680/ballistite

On September 30, 1938, British Prime Minister Neville Chamberlain hailed the Munich Agreement with Hitler as being the achievement of "peace for our time." Standing outside his official residence at 10 Downing Street, Chamberlain said, "My good friends, this is the second time in our history that there has come back from Germany to Downing Street, peace with honour. I believe it is peace for our time. We thank you from the bottom of our hearts. And now I recommend you to go home and sleep quietly in your beds." The very next day, German forces marched on Sudetenland and from there went on to occupy Czechoslovakia. World War II had not been averted, and peace had not been won, through either intimidation or negotiation.

For most of this decade, more than fifty different wars and conflicts have been raging around the world during any given year. Hundreds of thousands of people have suffered violence, hunger, displacement, and death as the result. Even now, children are being enslaved or orphaned, women are being brutally raped, and countless civilian populations are suffering the excruciating physical and emotional traumas of war. In spite of unprecedented efforts by the United Nations to bring nations of the world together in working for peace and development on agreed principles of justice, human dignity, and the well-being of all people, the nations of the world have been unable to achieve peace in our time. Sixty-five years after the founding of the United Nations, with its emblem of the world encircled by two "olive branches of peace," peace itself remains an elusive and unrealized dream.

"Is a world without wars even possible?" asked the writer of an article on world peace. "If it is, it will be the mother of all miracles. If it isn't, [then] awarding the Nobel Peace Prize to anyone is a tragic joke." [3]

Most dictionaries define peace primarily as "the non-warring condition of a nation, a group of nations, or the world; or as an agreement or treaty between warring or antagonistic nations, groups, etc. to end hostilities and abstain from further fighting or antagonism." [4] By such definitions, peace is experienced in many places and peace has even been tenuously secured and ensured through violence and war. Yet as a universal human state of affairs, peace as the total absence of war and conflict in the world has never been experienced. We are quite possibly further from realizing world peace today than ever before.

There is much more to peace than the absence of conflict and the presence of peaceful coexistence. Peace is ultimately the experience of contentment, harmony, and a sense of personal well-being in our relationships with other people. For the past 2,000 years, indeed during most of human history, there has not been a significant period of time without war, peace has not overtaken the world, violence has not been vanquished! We live in an anguished, conflictive, and bloody world. Amid economic and political uncertainties and difficult relationships, we wage our

---

3   http://americandaily.com/index.php/article/2697

4   Webster's *New Universal Unabridged Dictionary* (Random House, 1996).

own personal battles against situations and people. We live in conflict more often than we live in peace.

"May the peace of the Lord be always with you," I say as I shake hands with the folks around me in church as we exchange "the peace." "And also with you," they respond. What is this peace of the Lord, this "peace on earth" that was predicted by the prophets and then announced at the birth of Jesus? There is something attractive about being delivered from war and violence by God coming into the world to vanquish the enemies of peace in order to establish His Kingdom as a new world order. Ironically, that is not what happened when Jesus was born. Even as the refrains of "peace on earth" echoed through the night, Jesus was born as a helpless baby in a hostile empire. His family became refugees when he was a child and, as a grown man, Jesus was subjected to ridicule, hostility, and rejection. Yet He lived and taught as a man of peace. He respected those who rejected Him, loved those who laughed at Him, and offered to forgive those who maligned and abused Him.

Fear is what makes both people and nations prone to fight. Jesus said, "Peace I leave with you; my peace I give you. I do not give to you as the world gives. Do not let your hearts be troubled and do not be afraid" (John 14:27). Jesus came into the world to show us the way, to lead us into peace, and to empower us to live in peace by His love for us. Peace is the miracle of hope born in the hearts of fearful, conflictive people like us through Jesus Christ.

Lord, make me an instrument of your peace;

where there is hatred, let me sow love;

where there is injury, pardon;

where there is doubt, faith;

where there is despair, hope;

where there is darkness, light;

and where there is sadness, joy.

O Divine Master,

grant that I may not so much seek to be consoled as to console;

to be understood, as to understand;

to be loved, as to love;

for it is in giving that we receive,

it is in pardoning that we are pardoned,

and it is in dying that we are born to Eternal Life.[5]

---

5   Prayer attributed to St Francis.

CHAPTER 36

SACRED IN THE PROFANE

It was early in the winter season and the accumulated snow was unusually deep, loose, and fluffy, burying the scrubby brush high up on the Cape Breton Highlands. A friend and I decided to snowshoe across the highlands and then down the mountainside to my home on the shore. What seemed like a good plan at the outset soon turned into a painful and dangerous struggle as we constantly broke through the thin, icy crust into the deep, loose snow covering the bush. In exhaustion and frustration, I cursed the very snow whose beauty I had admired just hours before. This was absolutely not the idyllic excursion into the winter wonderland that either of us had envisioned.

I felt like cursing, as much at the snow as at myself, as I struggled through waist-deep snow, trying desperately to gain a footing on the thin crust. "I hate this blinking white crap," I shouted just seconds later as I broke through and sank into the deep snow for at least the hundredth time. Without moving, I cursed the snow and the unseen bushes underneath that entangled my snowshoes. Frustration and anger replaced my enjoyment of the day's beauty and my sense of the Creator's presence within me and around me.

I did not stop to think of what I was really saying or doing at the time but, in looking back, I see how often I revert into profanity. I don't understand why the tendency to curse at inconveniences and failures comes so easily to me. Yet the profanity of others greatly bothers me because it spoils and mars the good space between us. Often I will laugh to relieve the tension, but it is not something that laughter can cover up, nor would any objection I voice undo or repair it.

There are men and women whose ethos of life is profanity in speech and style. Often in conversation with prisoners and ex-prisoners I make a point of listening to their life stories, journeys through pain, prison, and profanity into a discovery of grace and beauty. These are miraculous stories of redemption, transformation, and restoration, stories of profanity undone by the mercy and love of Jesus, who broke through the profanity of the world, bringing peace, joy, and beauty into their lives and relationships.

The Easter story of Jesus' death and resurrection mirrors the Exodus story of the deliverance and restoration of the people of God from bondage. Like the Exodus story, the Easter story is marred with human profanity in word and deed. Peter,[1] one of Jesus' closest disciples, lets loose with a string of profanity and denial when, for a third time, he is accused of being associated with Jesus. In sheer fear, Peter reacts to the accusation with a string of curses so as to distance himself from Jesus. But even as the curses

---

1 *The Sacred and Profane* by Mircea Eliade (Harcourt Inc., Orlando FL, 1959– p. 14).

leave his mouth he realizes his folly. In the very moment of profanity, Jesus bridges the distance between them with a look of love that causes Peter to break down and weep in awareness that Jesus' love is present in the face of his profanity, his deepest fears, frustration, and anger (Mark 14:70-72).

During the crucifixion of Jesus, two other prisoners cringed and cried out in the excruciating cruelty of their final hours. One of them hurled insult upon insult at Jesus, giving vent to his anger, fear, and suffering. The air was filled with the crass profanity of mocking soldiers and spectators accompanying the bitter defiance of a tortured prisoner. But even then, the second of the two prisoners realized that the space between himself and Jesus was a sacred space; instead of profanity, he pled for pardon and for grace. Jesus embraced him within the profane and tortured space they shared, transforming inhumanity and evil with grace and hope (Luke 23:35-43).

There are just two modes of being in the world, two ways of seeing and interacting with life, the sacred and the profane. Profanity is defined by abuse, irreverence, or contempt, debasing or demeaning something or someone through vulgarity. For many people, life has no inherent meaning apart from their own physical, social and emotional gratification. For some people, life as they know it in the here and now is all there is or ever will be—for others life has a sacred meaning, life is not just physical and social but also spiritual. The process of living is not just personal and interpersonal but a process of communion with God.

Their life is a sacrament inasmuch as it is a physical or visible expression of a spiritual reality.

I know that there is no dividing line between the sacred and the temporal. Everything has been created by God for good. Through our participation in profanity, the space between ourselves and God, and the space between us and others, becomes tarnished and demeaned. And yet, even in the resounding echoes of our own profanity we stand beside Peter looking into the loving eyes of Jesus; in the spasms of our own pain and frustration, we raise our eyes to see Jesus looking at us with great affection, suffering with us, embracing us, blessing us, and transforming us by His grace.

BEANNACHT
("Blessing")

On the day when
the weight deadens
on your shoulders
and you stumble,
may the clay dance
to balance you.

And when your eyes
freeze behind
the grey window
and the ghost of loss
gets in to you,
may a flock of colours,
indigo, red, green,
and azure blue
come to awaken in you
a meadow of delight.

When the canvas frays
in the currach of thought
and a stain of ocean
blackens beneath you,
may there come across the waters
a path of yellow moonlight
to bring you safely home.[2]

2 By the late Irish poet, John O'Donohue.

154

Chapter 37

FAITH AND FISHER FOLK

Fish is my food of choice. While I've sometimes enjoyed being able to catch my own fish, I just don't have the time and patience that fishing takes, especially when it comes to cleaning the catch.

I've always wondered why Jesus chose fishermen to be his first disciples and why he entrusted them to be apostles of the good news. Is there something about fishermen that makes them especially receptive to redemption, discipleship, and leadership?

Every year as the lobster season opens, I eagerly anticipate our first feed of lobsters fresh from the sea. Lobster fishing is demanding and sometimes dangerous work. Not a season goes by without one or more fishermen losing their lives in the treacherous North Atlantic waters. For many years the courage and costs associated with fishing have been rewarded with plentiful catches and good profits, but it is not always a sure thing. None of the fishermen know for certain how they will fare at the beginning of each season.

During a sailing voyage a few years ago, a fellow sailor and I encountered a fierce storm that caused us to seek safe haven in the port of Ballantyne's Cove, home to a once-bustling, bluefin tuna fishery. In a nearby museum, photos of enormous tuna weighing over 500 kilograms (1,200 pounds) and descriptions of exciting fish-tales depicted a bygone era when the tuna were plentiful and when fishermen in small boats and simple gear braved the sea, risking everything in search of the valuable tuna. However, today the bluefin tuna fishery is virtually depleted. Only a few remaining diehard, tenacious fishermen persist in fishing.

What got me thinking about fishermen and the state of the fishery was news that the Sea of Galilee was being closed to all fishing.[1] It is the end of an era for fishers who, since before the time of Jesus, have maintained the fishing way of life. I thought back to the stories of Jesus walking the shores and sailing on the waters of Galilee with His fishermen disciples. How things have changed since then. I wonder what would happen if Jesus were walking the shores of Galilee or Ballantyne's Cove, or any of the fishing ports of the world, today. Who would He call to follow Him if all the fisher folk are gone? Could Jesus still cause the empty nets of weary and discouraged fishers to become overloaded with teeming fish, even though the waters of the world are polluted and the fish stocks decimated? Would any of the remaining fishermen, frustrated and exhausted by catching nothing, heed the advice of Jesus to throw their nets to the other side of the boat? I wonder what the Man from Galilee would be saying to us as we find ourselves working in unproductive and polluted areas, whether as fishermen, farmers, office workers, or in the marketplaces of the world.

---

1   http://news.bbc.co.uk/2/hi/8675076.stm

If Jesus called ordinary fisher folk to be His ambassadors back then, I suspect that He is calling ordinary struggling people like you and me to be ambassadors of good news in the world today.

THE MAN FROM GALILEE
Put your hand in the hand of the man
who stilled the water.
Put your hand in the hand of the man
who calmed the sea.
Take a look at yourself
and you can look at others differently
by putting your hand in the hand of
the man from Galilee.
Mama taught me how to pray
before I reached the age of seven
When I am down on my knees that's
when I feel close to Heaven.
Daddy lived his life
with two kids and a wife
you do what you must do
but he showed me enough of
what it takes to get me through.

By putting my hand in the hand of the man
who stilled the waters
putting my hand in the hand of the man
who calmed the seas
I took a look at myself and I could
look at others differently,
Because I put my hand in the hand
of the man from Galilee.

Every time I look into the holy book
I want to tremble
When I read about the part where
the carpenter cleared the temple.
For the buyers and sellers
were no different fellers than
what I profess to be
and it causes me shame to know
we're not the people we should be.

We need to put our hands in the hand
of the man who stilled the waters
put our hands in the hands
of the man who calmed the seas
We need to take a look at ourselves
and then we can look at others differently
by putting our hands in the hand
of the man from Galilee.[2]

---

2   *"Put Your Hand in the Hand."* A gospel song composed by Gene MacLellan and first recorded by Canadian singer Anne Murray.

CHAPTER 38

PRESENCE IN THE SILENCE

Some silence is good while other silence can be bad. Bad silence is when a difference of opinion turns into an argument that degenerates into an unyielding stand-off as two people turn away and refuse to speak to each other. Bad silence is returning home at night and the normal sounds are gone. There is nothing, just empti-ness. Somebody is missing. Bad silence is when something needs to be said yet, because of shared fear, no one has the courage to speak. Bad silence can be the ominous calm before the storm, when even the breeze and the leaves in the trees stop whispering and the birds are still. Bad silence is waiting for a call to be returned by a friend, but the call does not come.

Good silence is the warm and welcome space between two people whose love for one another goes beyond the reach of words. Good silence is the stillness of an early-morning hour when all creation wakens to the glory of its Creator. Good silence is the holding of one's tongue instead of making sport of someone else, absorbing criticism with-out defense, deflecting anger with a smile, and keeping the confidence of a friend. Good silence is not being inclined to top the story of another person even when you can.

Good silence is the anticipation of God's presence in quiet moments amid the tumult of the day. Good silence is the prayer of waiting to hear from God when impatient thoughts and pressing needs agitate one's heart and soul. Good silence is the joyful, creative, hopeful, and peaceful sense of being surrounded and upheld in the presence of Christ.

As contemporary believers, we have much to learn from some of the spiritual traditions and practices of previous eras. The Benedictine spiritual tradition begins with an invitation to "listen with the ear of your heart." Benedict knew that belonging to God involves being attuned to and listening for God's voice in the silence, as well as learning and living out the truths of the faith. Those who listen to voices other than God tend to build their identity elsewhere, instead of in a responsive relationship with Him. Silence is considered one of the cornerstones of spiritual development, but the goal of silence lies not in simply refraining from talking. Silence is rooted in respect for others, a sense of place, a spirit of peace, and thoughtful conversation. The practice of silence merely as an end in itself or for wrong reasons—like insulating silence or silence that is passive-aggressive, or even silence that is insensitive to the presence and needs of others—is not the kind of silence by which the believer becomes attuned and attentive to the "word of the Lord."

But how does one find or create that inner silence in a world bombarded with incessant messages and demand-

ing communications? Years ago, during a time less tumul-
tuous than our own, T. S. Eliot voiced his own yearning
for silence: "Where shall the word be found, where will
the word resound? Not here, there is not enough silence ...
The right time and the right place are not here. No place of
grace for those who avoid the face. No time to rejoice for
those who walk among the noise and deny the voice."

An ancient story is told about three brothers who visited
St Antony of Egypt, one of the most famous desert fathers.
During the course of their visits two of the brothers contin-
ually beleaguered St Antony with their incessant requests
for spiritual advice and words of wisdom to help them on
their journey of faith. The third brother always remained
silent during these visits. Then, during one of the visits, St
Antony turned to him, asking if he might not also have a
request like his brothers. To this the quiet brother simply
replied, "It is enough for me that I am with you, Father."

> *They tell me, Lord, that when I seem*
> > *To be in speech with you,*
> *Since but one voice is heard, it's all a dream,*
> > *One talker aping two.*
> *Sometimes it is, yet not as they*
> > *Conceive it, Rather, I*
> *Seek in myself the things I hoped to say,*
> > *But lo!, my wells are dry.*
> *Then, seeing me empty, you forsake*
> > *The listener's role and through*
> *My dumb lips breathe and into utterance wake*
> > *The thoughts I never knew.*

And thus you neither need reply
Nor can; thus, while we seem
Two talkers, thou art One forever, and I
No dreamer, but thy dream.

C.S. Lewis, *Letters to Malcolm* pages 67-8

Chapter 39

WHAT'S IN A STORM?

For nearly three days we watched and waited as Hurricane Bill (a tropical cyclone) churned its way northward over the open waters of the Atlantic. It is not often that storms of this magnitude make it all the way from the Caribbean to our island off the northeast coast of Nova Scotia. But Bill was expected to make landfall with torrential rain and fierce, tropical, storm-force winds. Already the sultry air was dripping with humidity. The sky was darkening even while the wind remained ominously calm. Long, surging waves were thundering rhythmically against the shoreline as a drum roll for what was yet to come.

We were as prepared as we could possibly be for stormy weather. I actually enjoy a good storm; not the damage that storms can do, but the uninhibited drama and unleashed passion in nature's awesome power seems to me a spectacular display of the Creator's power. I realize that God often gets blamed for natural disasters, "acts of God" in the language of many people. While I have no satisfying spiritual explanation for the devastation that some storms cause, I don't really believe that God deliberately directs the path of every storm or that God's power is the power of the storm.

There are more lessons to be learned in storms than from calm and pleasant weather. In the world of ship-building and boat design, a vessel is not considered seaworthy until it has been thoroughly tested under adverse storm conditions. Inevitably, more is learned about the seaworthiness of a vessel's design, its sailing characteristics, and the dependability of its structure and systems through testing it on stormy seas than on placid water. It is equally interesting that storms also bring out the best and worst in people. Some of the most unlikely people courageously risk themselves to help those in need or danger, while some of the most likely people retreat into cowardice to save their own skin and possessions.

Jesus told a poignant storm story to help people understand that spiritual integrity is like the structural integrity of a house; it depends on a solid foundation (Matt. 7:24-27). The principles of engineering and architectural design in constructing a house are meaningless unless they are applied from the ground up. Likewise, a person's life will not ultimately endure the storms of life unless the teachings of Jesus are applied from the ground up in daily living.

We can understand how a person born into extreme poverty, or who has been socially and sexually victimized, or emotionally ravaged by conflict and injustice, ends up leading a life of criminality and addiction. Yet we find it difficult to understand how an educated, successful, respected person in the community can descend into criminality and addiction. During my visits to prison I have met both kinds of men and women, who have told me of reaching a breaking point as the result of severe and often sustained financial, social, or emotional storms converging into a "perfect storm." Their fragile moral and spiritual underpinnings could not stand up to the sustained duress of storms, and their entire lives collapsed in ruin.

As Hurricane Bill approached and the rain intensified, I became aware of several leaks in the roof of our house. But the testing point of the storm is not just about the storm-worthiness of our roof, it is about the foundations and structural integrity of the building. The storm brings a lesson of faith for, like the disciples of Jesus, my faith seems solid when the hungry poor are fed, when the homeless and the sick are cared for, when justice is done, and when enthusiastic people sing in joyful adoration of Jesus. And yet, like the disciples, the storm-worthiness of my faith is often put to the test when I am overtaken by a storm of unexpected magnitude, of whatever kind.

When Jesus had miraculously satisfied the hunger of 5,000 people, and after the disciples had gathered baskets of leftovers evidencing God's amazing provision, and when the people wanted to make Jesus King in recognition of the abundance of food He had given them, at the end of that glorious faith-filled day the disciples learned that they could also depend on Jesus when they felt alone and beleaguered in the clutches of a frightful storm.

> ... the disciples went down to the lake, where they got into
> a boat and set off across the lake for Capernaum. By now
> it was dark, and Jesus had not yet joined them. A strong

wind was blowing and the waters grew rough. When they had rowed three or three and a half miles, they saw Jesus approaching the boat, walking on the water, and they were terrified. But he said to them, "It is I; don't be afraid." Then they were willing to take him into the boat, and immediately the boat reached the shore where they were heading (John 6:16-21).

CHAPTER 40

CENTERD IN THE STORM

We were under full sail and making good headway against a 15-knot wind. With gently rolling sea swells of a meter or less and a bright, blue sky fringed with lazy, white clouds, sailing conditions could not have been better for our offshore crossing from the island to a remote harbor on the mainland. As sight of land disappeared behind us, there was nothing but the sky and sea and the sound of the wind on our sails. It was glorious!

Several hours had passed when an odd edge to the wind aroused me from my reverie: just a few erratic puffs at first and then a slight easterly shift. Something didn't feel quite right to me as I scanned the horizon for telltale signs of a weather front. Far off in the distance I spotted an ominous low-lying, dark squall line punctuated by what seemed to be white water. "Let's reef the jib," I called out to my sailing partner. "There seems to be a bit of weather coming our way." Literally within the next thirty minutes, the sky grew completely overcast, the wind shifted precipitously to the southeast with gusts increasing to more than 25 knots, and the sea's rhythmic swells became a turbulent contradiction of two-meter waves crossing three to four-meter swells. Without having anticipated it, we were sailing directly into the shifting path of a dying, tropical storm. So much for marine weather forecasts!

Now we were sailing with only a storm jib and engine power as we struggled to maintain our course against the growing onslaught. It was wild, unlike any storm I've encountered on the sea, and I cried out to the Lord of land and sea to spare us from disaster. After several treacherous hours, we finally spotted the headland and a buoy marking the entrance to a small fishing harbor. It was all we could do to navigate our way through a narrow channel into the relative safety of the harbor. By the grace of God, we safely made it. All night long the storm persisted with winds inside the harbor topping 50 knots!

For weeks before this I had been pondering the experience of Jesus and His disciples who were overtaken by a sudden storm at sea. With the disciples in "all-hands-on-deck" mode, they were desperately fighting against the shrieking storm to keep the boat from capsizing. Jesus was sound asleep in the stern. I find the scene totally astounding, for I have never slept nor can I imagine anyone sleeping on a boat in the middle of a ferocious gale as the wind screams through the rigging and roiling waves toss the vessel about like a piece of cork. To sleep through something like that would be completely unnatural! Fear and desperation are the emotions people experience in a storm at sea. They are alert, not asleep. Certain that calamity was overtaking them, that they were about to drown, the fearful crew roused Jesus from sleep: "Lord save us! We're going to drown!"

Now that is a prayer I can relate to. Yet much to my astonishment, as I am sure it was to theirs, Jesus rebuked them for being afraid and for being men of "little faith." I am puzzled and irritated by Jesus' response. After all, the men cried out for the Lord to save them; they did not call for the Coastguard or another god. Doesn't that seem like the typical cry of faith? When they knew that all was lost and that there was nothing more that they could do to keep the boat afloat, they cried out to the Lord, and I have done the same (Matt. 8:23-27).

As I consider this story and my own experience, I ponder on what happened to them and what happens to me in the center of the storm. I think about what it is that centers me in the middle of the storm. Am I centered on impending calamity or on Jesus? I don't think that Jesus rebuked the men for waking Him up or even for crying out to Him in their distress. I think he rebuked them for being centered in their fear, for totally giving in to fear. They "knew" that all was lost and they were more certain of drowning than of deliverance, notwithstanding the fact that Jesus was in the boat with them.

In life, as on the sea, there are storms that can be predicted and those that come upon us as if out of nowhere. There are storms we can prepare for and those that catch us unaware. Prepared or not, we cannot always avoid the center of the storm. The assurance of faith in Jesus is not in avoiding the storm, but in the knowledge that He is in the center of the storm with us. Fear cannot overcome or supplant His presence in the center of the storm. There is a world of difference between being centered in fear or fate, and being centered in Jesus the Lord of all Creation—even of "perfect" storms at sea. The way of faith is centered in Jesus in the midst of anything that threatens to overcome us. To be centered in Jesus is to deny the storm its ultimate fright and might.

CHAPTER 41

THE END OF THE WORLD

One's destination is never a place, but rather a new way of looking at things.[1]

"This is the end of the world," my mother declared as my father turned the car down another long, rough, dusty, country road on our drive to visit friends we had not seen for a long time. I was young and understood her literally. "Why do they live here?" I asked, knowing that the end of the world must be a precipitously dangerous place. "Well, this isn't quite the end of the world," my father interjected. "But can we see it from here?" I asked. "What if I walk to the end of the field, is it there? Will I fall off if I get too close?"

In my small childhood world this was high adventure, pushing to the outer limits of the world as I knew it. I was eager to see what the end of the world looked like, to be first among my little friends to tell the story. Unfortunately, I never did reach the end of the world, and as the horizons of my knowledge expanded I came to know the difference between the literal meaning of words and figures of speech.

---

1 Henry Miller 1891-1980 (an American author) *Big Sur and the Oranges of Hieronymus Bosch.*

"Stop the world and let me get off!" I cried out, during my heady university days. In my rapidly expanding world of new ideas, experiences, and opportunities, it seemed like everything was changing, nothing was staying the same. Often I felt disoriented and lonely on a fathomless expanse of shifting values and mind-blowing possibilities. I was experiencing the end of the neatly ordered world of my youth. It was expanding into an exciting and beckoning new world without limits and without borders in which I felt a bit lost.

"My world has collapsed, my life is finished," begins a heart-wrenching refrain I hear from many prisoners. "Everything I had is gone: my family, home, money, even my reputation. There is nothing left of my world. I might as well be dead." Without a sense of destiny or hope, many prisoners become resigned to living in a collapsed and suffocating world of captivity. For them, the world outside of prison might just as well be a place of surreal nightmares and long-forgotten dreams. It is the end of the world as they knew it.

"This world is not my home, I'm just passing through," some Christians tell me as they lament the moral and spiritual state of the world. "I can't wait to get to heaven," I've heard some say as if their lives in the real world are just to be tolerated. I have often wondered why Jesus referred to the kingdom of heaven as being a nearby reality (Matt. 3:2, Luke 10:9) and why He talked about his followers being the light of the world if the only thing that really mattered was the end of the present world and the dawn of a distant, heavenly but coming kingdom.

"The end of the world is near—December 21, 2012 to be exact." [2] This was yet another doomsday prophecy derived from supposedly ancient Mayan predictions. In response to previous media hype about another "end of the world" prediction, a religious advertisement announced, "The Escape Plan," offering salvation for people fearful of, and unprepared for, the coming end of the world.

If the only destiny of the world were intended to be one of doom and destruction, I wonder why God even bothered Himself with its people and why those who follow Jesus are consigned to remain in the world. Why would Jesus have instructed those who follow Him to go to every part of the world to proclaim the Good News to the whole of creation? (Mark 16:15). And is this good news only a means of escaping from this world into a new and blissful world at the end of time? Could it be that the kingdom of heaven is not just a place or a destination, but that it is also a whole new way of seeing life in the present world? Could it be a radical new way of living life from the perspective of God's love, God the Creator who brought heaven and earth and everything in between into existence?

I am convinced that the end of the world as we know it comes when our perspective is transformed from one of self-interest, self-indulgence, self-promotion, and self-preservation, to seeing the world through the eyes of the One who did not seek to escape it but who loved the world so much that He came to make it better—to save it from

---

2 http://news.nationalgeographic.com/news/2009/11/091106-2012-end ...

itself. He entered the world as a friend of wrongdoers and miscreants, a seeker of the lost and confused, a healer of the diseased and afflicted; a liberator of captives and captors; a comforter for the mournful and the anguished, and as a refuge for all manner of harassed, hapless, and helpless people. He is Jesus, the One who transforms our world and our lives by His love; who leads us not in a way of escaping the world, but into a new perspective on our place and purpose in the world.

> *Jesus said,*
> *"My prayer is not that you take them out of the world*
>   *but that you protect them from the evil one ...*
> *As you sent me into the world, I have sent them into the*
>   *world."* (John 17:15, 18)

CHAPTER 42

HEART OF DARKNESS

It was an unspeakable horror; as inhumane, unjust, and evil as I had ever encountered. The photos and report graphically portrayed the suffering of prisoners throughout the country. "The State is locking them up in hellholes, condemning them to slow starvation and possibly death from nutrition-related illnesses or the vast array of other diseases they are exposed to through unhygienic conditions. Despite terrible desperation, their position as 'prisoners' means they are denied the most basic human instinct and that is to fight for survival ... Extreme hunger, inhumane, squalid conditions, exposure to a variety of diseases and stripping people of their dignity are standard practices ... resulting in shameful misery hidden away from the public gaze behind high walls and razor wire." [1]

I had been inside those very prisons and come face to face with the heart of human darkness. I saw the reality of evil, not only in the lives of bitter, hardened criminals, but in the actions of people in power who condoned and perpetrated injustice and inhumanity, and in the clean hands of people who knew what was happening but refused to act.

---

1 http://www.sokwanele.com/thisiszimbabwe/archives/3882

Bystanders are complicit with perpetrators of evil if they do nothing to resist it.[2] Just as the world became complicit in Rwanda's genocide by refusing to intervene, so too are we whenever we avert our eyes from evil and refrain from exposing or acting to restrain it. Yet there are situations in which it seems that there is little we can do against pervasive evil and its overwhelming power. Whenever I encounter such seemingly intractable situations, I am reminded of St Paul's observation that "...our struggle is not against flesh and blood, but against the rulers, against the powers, against the world forces of this darkness, against the spiritual forces of wickedness in the heavenly places" (Eph. 6:12 NASB). How else can I or anyone else explain the horrific nature of evil in the world, not only the evil inherent in the perpetrators but in complicit bystanders?

How can we explain the actions of relief organizations that collect huge donations to bring aid to people suffering disaster and starvation but refuse to help starving, dying prisoners because "they don't deserve" to be helped? How can we explain the rationale of governments that are more concerned about public perceptions than about humanitarian relief if they supply food aid for starving prisoners. "Why are you doing this for convicted prisoners," they ask, "and not for starving children in other countries with just as much need for food?" Yet whether it is starving children or starving parents in prison, the starvation and the suffer-

---

2 "All that is necessary for evil to triumph is for good men to stand by and do nothing" Edmund Burke, British politician and philosopher 1729-1797.

ing are real, as real as the evil that keeps these good people and organizations from doing the right thing. This is the heart of darkness.

It is inevitable that in following Jesus we will be confronted with the heart of darkness, the reality of evil in the world. During Jesus' final days on earth all of the forces of evil conspired against Him. He was faced with political oppression and injustice, cultural alienation and violence, religious scapegoating and exclusion, social betrayal and abandonment, personal agony, and death! All facets of evil massed to push Him over the brink of God-denial, despair, and destruction ... and failed.

As an innocent man, brutalized and condemned to death by the powers that be, Jesus confronted evil to overcome it by taking, absorbing, and exhausting it, in order that there will be a new creation, a new covenant, forgiveness, freedom, and hope. By His refusal to capitulate to evil, by His courage to remain true to God, by absorbing every abuse and agony that evil could muster against Him—even death—Jesus conquered the power of evil. As followers of Jesus, we accompany Him into the heart of the darkness of our world, confronting evil with goodness, truth, and hope in the power of His resurrection. Even in the face of death, evil is not the final word.

> *Be ye steadfast - In yourselves.*
>> *Unmovable - By others;*
>> *continually increasing in the work of faith*
>>> *and labour of love. Knowing your labour*
>>> *is not in vain in the Lord –*

Whatever ye do for his sake shall have its full

reward in that day. Let us also endeavour, by

cultivating holiness in all its branches,

to maintain this hope in its full energy;

longing for that glorious day,

when, in the utmost extent of the expression,

death shall be swallowed up for ever,

and millions of voices, after the long silence of the

grave,

shall burst out at once into that triumphant song,

O death, where is thy sting?

O Hades, where is thy victory? [3]

---

3   John Wesley's notes on 1 Corinthians 15:55-58 – http://www.ccel.org/ccel/
wesley/notes.titlepage.html

CHAPTER 43

THE MORE THINGS CHANGE ...

Something in the very nature of change resists the process of change, even when that change is for good. Change is inherently difficult and the greater the change and its implications, the more likely it is that the change itself will remain an unrealized idea or desire. It has often been observed rather cynically that "the more things change, the more they stay the same." [1]

Yet change is often the claim championed by political foes during election campaigns. More often than not, the "what" and "how" of the change they propose to bring about are not clear. As voters we sometimes wonder what it will take to produce a significant change for good and if significant changes are even within the realm of political possibility.

During many conversations with criminal offenders around the world, I've talked extensively about change: behavioral, attitudinal, and lifestyle, as well as moral and spiritual change. Often, even when the need for change is evident, many offenders resign themselves to the "impossi-

---

1 A saying of French origin that seems to have been first used by French novelist Alphonse Karr and by the Irish playwright George Bernard Shaw who used the phrase in *Revolutionist's Handbook* (1903).

bility" of ever changing. "I've tried, but it doesn't work," is the usual refrain "Everything is stacked against me." And there are others who have been serious about change. "When I get out of prison, I'm never coming back," they declare. "I'm going to turn my life around this time for sure." And yet most of them fail and eventually return to prison.

Real change originates from the inside out, not from the outside in. A change in political power can no more produce a deep social reformation than a change in prison conditions can transform a criminal mind. Personal change for good begins with moral reorientation, a basic change in the value system of a person. The real cultural and social reformation of a society begins within the spirituality of its people; a fundamental inner change of life perspective and values, not an outer change of political realignment, economic readjustment, or legislative changes.

Change for good begins with an inner not an outer change. As so many criminal offenders, drug addicts, and sexual predators have come to realize, none of us can ultimately transform ourselves by ourselves. We don't have the power. Inner change is neither self-generated nor self-sustained. One of the ancient prophets said it best when he declared that even as a leopard is unable to change its spots, so it is impossible for a person steeped in doing evil to become good (Jer. 13:23). Another of the prophets said that only God can replace the stone-cold heart of a person with a new and lively desire for good (Ezek. 36:25-27).

The more things change the more they stay the same, at least when people presume to live as the captains of their own souls and masters of their own fate.[2] That is not to say that any of us should not work at being good and doing good. But the starting point is to realize that we cannot change ourselves for good by decisive will or through creative efforts alone, nor can we reform our culture through more political effort or legislative mandate.

Humanity as a whole, and people as individuals, will inevitably decline in ever-downward circles apart from the grace and power of our ever-loving Creator, who made us for good. And when we tried to help ourselves He sent Jesus to save us from both our feeblest and our best efforts to help ourselves. Change is possible and through Him the heart of change is the heart of the person, the heart of society.

> *Do not conform any longer to the pattern of this world,*
> *but be transformed by the renewing of your*
> > *mind.* (Rom. 12:2)

> *... because of His great love for us,*
> *God, who is rich in mercy,*
> *made us alive with Christ even when we were dead in*
> > *transgressions ...*
> *For it is by grace you have been saved, through faith—*
> *and this not from yourselves,*
> *it is the gift of God.* (Eph. 2:4, 8)

---

2   "It matters not how strait the gate, how charged with punishments the scroll, I am the master of my fate, I am the captain of my soul." (from the poem *"Invictus"* by William Ernest Henley, 1875).

Part F

The Way of Jesus: Living Radically

Chapter 44

THE POLITICS OF JESUS

I grew up in a small town where the Christian faith was very much the status quo. It was on leaving home to study at the university in a city far from home that I began thinking critically about my faith. University studies opened my mind to broader horizons. I faced new social and intellectual challenges through which the notions of my small-town faith were assailed by the overwhelming logic of science and reason.

Although I did not completely turn away from the Jesus I had grown up with, my faith in Him became less relevant within the pragmatic realities of academic and social pursuit. I also became passionately involved in the compelling social issues of war and poverty, injustice, and inequality, and expressed my new-found passion in the politics of student protest. We rallied against the war in Vietnam, American imperialism, moral and political authority, and the very notion of capitalism. We were going to change the world! My heroes of the day were outspoken leaders of social revolution, and included the likes of Cesar Chavez, Che Guevara, and Martin Luther King. To me these leaders seemed far more relevant and were making a greater difference in the world than either the religion or the 'churchified' Jesus of my small-town faith.

One day, as I was walking through a student lounge, a glaring poster caught my attention. "Christ the Revolutionary!" it proclaimed in huge red letters, followed by details of a special lecture by a visiting campus minister. I chuckled to myself, ridiculing the notion of Jesus being revolutionary in any sense of the word. Yet my curiosity and cynicism were piqued to the point that I could not resist going to the lecture.

I remember next to nothing about the presentation, but by the time I left that lecture hall I was awakening to a realization that Jesus Christ is the most revolutionary person who ever lived. He lived a revolutionary way of non-violent love and forgiveness in the face of injustice and in the depths of the human condition. The ways of all the other revolutionary leaders I could think of were characterized by angry confrontation, incendiary rhetoric, and violent actions aimed at forcing changes and overthrowing political powers. It was the day I began seeing Jesus Christ in a new way. Over time he became more real and more compelling than any of my revolutionary heroes.

I began to see how the life and message of Jesus was a radical challenge to the established political and religious order of His day. Jesus lived and walked among the poor, the despised, and forsaken. Everywhere he went, needy and curious people crowded close to Him. His demonstration and proclamation of God's love and the good news of God's Kingdom was met with great expectation by a society chafing under the yoke of Roman imperialism.

People yearned for Jesus to do for them and for their subjugated nation what no other political leader or freedom fighter had been able to do. On a day when they thought those hopes were going to be realized, their jubilation knew no bounds. As Jesus rode into Jerusalem, the gathering crowd began shouting triumphantly and carpeting His royal way into the city with their coats and palm branches (Mark 11:8-10).

Ironically, in their enthusiasm the crowds seemed to overlook the fact that Jesus wasn't riding a stately steed, but a nondescript little donkey. Their expectations quickly become unglued as Jesus refused to grasp the momentum of the moment. He didn't confront the imperialistic Roman rulers. He didn't plant the national flag of God's Kingdom and His people, and at the end of the day nothing at all had changed. Jubilation gave way to bitter disappointment and, making things even worse, the religious leaders turned against Him. The same Jesus they heralded as the liberating king one day became their public enemy number one the next. Within days, they turned on Him and had Him arrested on charges of treason and sedition.

By the time Jesus stood for trial, He had been interrogated, tortured, and was considered a traitor by His disillusioned countrymen. By the politics of inflammatory accusation there was no longer a place for Him except execution. The Kingdom of God and the end of Roman imperialism would surely have to come by another leader, at another time, and in another way.

The situation culminated in the choice people had to make between Jesus of Nazareth and a notorious prisoner whose name was also Jesus—Jesus Barabbas,[1] a revolutionary leader, an insurrectionist, and freedom fighter in the Jewish resistance to Roman occupation. It was left to the people to side with one or the other Jesus. "Which one do you want me to release to you: Jesus Barabbas, or Jesus who is called Christ?" demanded Pilate. Their choice was overwhelming, if not unanimous, "Give us Jesus Barabbas." And with that, the people got what they wanted. What happened after that is history, a history that repeats itself again and again as people choose one Jesus over another, one revolutionary way over another (Matt. 27:15-26).

I came very close to choosing the violent way of Jesus Barabbas, the freedom fighter and insurrectionist, instead of the truly revolutionary way of Jesus Christ, who turns the world upside down, forgiving the unforgivable, loving the unlovable, and bringing life out of death. Every day I am still confronted with that choice of which Jesus to follow in petty, personal conflicts and disagreements, in facing people who don't care what happens to prisoners,

---

1 Matthew 27:17—early Greek manuscripts indicate that Barabbas' name was actually Jesus Barabbas. This is reflected in recent Bible translations of Matthew 27:17, including the New Revised Standard (NRSV), Today's New International Version (NIV), and New American Bible (NAB). According to the United Bible Societies' text, Matthew 27:17 reads: "... whom will ye that I release unto you? Jesus Barabbas [Greek: Iesous ton Barabban] or Jesus which is called Christ (Iesous ton legomenon Christon)?" Some early Syriac manuscripts of Matthew present Barabbas' name twice as Jesus bar Abbas: manuscripts in the Caesarean group of texts, the Sinaitic Palimpsest, the Palestinian Syriac lectionaries, and some of the manuscripts used by Origen in the third century, all support the fact that Barabbas' name was originally Jesus Barabbas (ref. Cambridge Encyclopedia).

in reacting to systemic injustice, in coming up against self-serving powers that heartlessly overlook the poor, and in my deep desire to make a difference in this corrupt and callous world.

> *The calling to which Jesus Christ has called,*
> *in virtue of the Lord's example,*
> *in virtue of the order of love,*
> *is on the side of the little people, the poor.*
> *His place in the world is there –*
> *the only place the way of love leads to.*
> *Even if he does not deliberately choose this place,*
> *he is there because his communion with Jesus Christ*
> *is communion with the Poor One*
> *who knew total poverty, total injustice, total*
>   *violence.*
> *When the Christian consciously keeps faith with his*
>   *Lord,*
> *he is led to the least of these,*
> *the brethren of the Lord,*
> *and to the Lord Himself.* [2]

---

2 Jacques Ellul, *The Politics of God and the Politics of Man* (Eerdmans, USA; 1972).

CHAPTER 45

THE SIGNATURE OF JESUS

Signatures were inscribed in ink all over the white linen tablecloth—famous names like Lech Walesa, Józef Glemp, Jerzy Popieluszko, and Karol Józef Wojtyla, as well as many names I could neither recognise nor pronounce. At one time or another, each one of those persons had been a dinner guest at this very table, and by their signatures it seemed to me that they were present with us now.

Seldom have I enjoyed a meal and found conversation as meaningful and stimulating as in the parish rectory of Msgr Jan Sikorski, of Warsaw, Poland, just months before the collapse of Communism. During our conversation around the table, I could almost feel the passion of history in the making and sense the presence of our unseen dinner companions, who had dared to stand for freedom, justice, and truth.

"Here, take this pen and write your name," Msgr Sikorski said graciously, offering me a pen as the evening meal came to an end. I hesitated, feeling myself an outsider and unworthy of adding my name to the illustrious company of heroes, saints, and martyrs. "You are one of us, a special guest at our table," he continued, sensing my reticence. The truth is that I actually did feel at home as we had

talked of many things, including Msgr Sikorski's courageous venture into prison chaplaincy and my involvement
with suffering prisoners in difficult prison systems around
the world. Finally, I signed my name in an open space on
the tablecloth. "But there seems to be a name missing," I
suggested, handing back his pen. "I don't see the signature
of Jesus on this tablecloth."

"Oh, He is always here," responded Msgr Sikorski without hesitation. "He is our host. His signature is on our lives,
not on the tablecloth." My mind raced back in time, visual-
izing a small plaque with an inscription that my mother
kept on the wall of the dining room in our house when I
was growing up. It read, "Christ is the head of this house,
the unseen guest at every meal, the silent listener to every
conversation." It had not meant much to me during my
youth, other than serving as a reminder not to say things
that weren't true or nice, or argue with my sister during
mealtimes.

The memory of that wonderful meal during my first visit
to Poland struck me with new force as I read and thought
about Jesus' final meal with His disciples (Matt. 26:17-30).
I visualized myself being seated at the table with them when,
towards the end of the meal, Jesus picked up a loaf of bread
and shared it with all of them saying, "This is my body given
for you, do this in remembrance of me."[1] Jesus was clearly
the host; He had invited us. We were all at the table because
of our relationship with Him. As usual it was a wonderful

---

1 http://christianityinview.com/eucharist.html

meal, not only because it satisfied our need for food but because it satisfied our deeper hunger for friendship and fellowship. Coming together for a meal was more about being with each other, more about Jesus inviting us to join Him for dinner and into His life, than it was about food and wine— although the food was superb and the vintage extraordinary.

That is the thing about dinner invitations. Whenever we invite, or are invited, to dinner, we recognize that it isn't primarily about the food. Behind every invitation to share a meal is the personal invitation to share life and friendship. The real life-giving nourishment during that last meal with Jesus was Jesus sharing His hospitality, giving Himself to His friends. "Do this," he said, "in remembrance of me." And I am sure that every time thereafter that His friends shared a meal together, Jesus was present among them, not because His name was written on their tablecloth, but because in breaking the bread and drinking the wine and sharing their lives with each other, they could not help but remember Jesus and talk about their experience and relationship with Him.

To this very day, followers of Jesus re-enact the last meal Jesus shared with His disciples before His arrest and crucifixion. The Last Supper has been as memorialized in art as in the traditions and teaching of the Church. Despite widely differing views and practices concerning the symbolic or literal meaning of Jesus' words about the bread being His body and the wine being His blood, what remains true for all believers is the spiritual nourishment we find in the presence of Jesus when we share a meal with Him.

Jesus is indeed our host. His signature is not on the tablecloth or the wine label or on the bread-wrapper, but on the lives of those who follow Him. He is the one who invites us not merely to share a meal, but to share His life and presence, to be renewed and strengthened to do the radically transforming, reconciling, and healing work He has given us to do in the world.

> *I am the Bread of life,*
> *He who comes to Me shall not hunger,*
> *He who believes in Me shall not thirst.*
> *No one can come to Me*
> *Unless the Father draw him.*
> *And I will raise him up,*
> *And I will raise him up,*
> *And I will raise him up on the last day.*
> *The bread that I will give*
> *Is My flesh for the life of the world,*
> *And he who eats of this bread,*
> *He shall live forever,*
> *He shall live forever.*
> *And I will raise him up,*
> *And I will raise him up,*
> *And I will raise him up on the last day.*
> *Unless you eat*
> *Of the flesh of the Son of Man*
> *And drink of His blood,*
> *And drink of His blood,*
> *You shall not have life within you.*
> *And I will raise him up,*
> *And I will raise him up,*

And I will raise him up on the last day.
I am the Resurrection,
I am the Life,
He who believes in Me
Even if he die,
He shall live forever.
And I will raise him up,
And I will raise him up,
And I will raise him up on the last day.
Yes, Lord, we believe
That You are the Christ,
The Son of God
Who has come
Into the world.
And I will raise him up,
And I will raise him up,
And I will raise him up on the last day.[2]

---

2   *I am the Bread of Life.* Lyrics by Suzanne Toolan.

CHAPTER 46

JESUS AND HUMAN ANGUISH

"Anguish," says Jean Vanier, "is the common experience of what it means to be human." We are finite beings and even the most powerful among us is incapable of fully controlling our lives and our existence. We are subject to experiences and conditions that we can neither understand nor overcome by the strength of our own will or effort. People in prison, victims of crime, and those who are forced out of their families, homes, and countries by violence or disaster know the face of anguish amid helplessness, pain, and fear.

For most of us, the anguish we feel may not be as visible as that of prisoners, yet we are so very familiar with anguish that only finds its painful expression through our tears:

Tears of love lost and love spurned
Tears of guilt and regret, of things done and left undone
Tears of embarrassment and humiliation
Tears of pain borne and pain inflicted
Tears of frustration and failure
Tears of loss and of being lost
Tears of bitter disappointment
Tears of uncertainty and dread
Tears of helplessness and fear
Tears of sympathy
Tears of anger
Tears!

We experience excruciating anguish in situations where comforting words offered by those around us do nothing to assuage those tears. Mere words cannot bandage or heal the wounds of humanity, and so we weep for ourselves and we weep with those who weep.[1] "Blessed are those who mourn," said Jesus, "for they will be comforted" (Matt. 5:4). Those who bear the anguish of others by their tears and by their silent presence are indeed more blessed than those who shrug their shoulders and walk away. Yet the inescapable reality of our humanity is that even by our tears we cannot save ourselves or others from the anguish of human brokenness. Left to ourselves we are exiled in a dark place of helplessness and hopelessness.

From that ancient time when our human story took us outside of the "garden" of God's companionship, humanity has been in anguish and captivity to pain: of childbearing; competing for survival against the thorns and thistles of life; and of suffering death's inevitable sting (Gen. 3:16-19). Through deception and destruction, calamity, and captivity, our human story continues to be written in the lives of people and nations. There is nothing that can rewrite this story or bring it to a better end. We live in anguish; that is our human story.

But for those who put their faith and trust in God, the end of our story is not in human anguish. Along with those who yearned for the coming of the Savior, so too we yearn for the Savior who will come again to wipe away all tears and put an end to death itself (Rev. 21:4). For He is the

---

1   Romans 12:15.

Savior of the world who radically assumes our infirmities and suffering, who carries our burdensome sorrow, and who bears the brutal consequences of our waywardness and wrongdoing.

He alone will deliver us from all anguish and bring us into peace.

> *Surely he took up our pain*
> *And bore our suffering*
> *yet we considered him punished by God,*
> *stricken by him and afflicted.*
> *But he was pierced for our transgressions*
> *he was crushed for our iniquities;*
> *the punishment that brought us peace was on him,*
> *and by his wounds we are healed.* (Isaiah 53:4, 5 NIV)

CHAPTER 47

JESUS: ONE OF US AND MORE

"You have no idea what it's really like being locked up like us, do you? Its hell and, buddy, if you haven't done the time don't waste mine," snarled a burly prisoner menacingly, the tattoos on his neck bulging as he spat out the words. "You're not one of us. What gives you the right to say anything!"

How often I have heard words to this effect during my prison visits, especially when I first began going to prisons. I quickly learned to be honest and now I always begin with a confession: "I don't know what it's like to be in prison, I've never been a prisoner. I don't know what it's like to be separated from family and friends, or what it feels like to be stuck in a place like this, completely helpless when things are going wrong at home. I have no idea what it's like to be facing years of confinement and a dismal future. The truth is that most of us on the outside haven't a clue what you are going through and, to make matters worse, most people don't care. They'd just as soon lock you up and throw the key away!'

Words like that usually get the attention of prison inmates and then I move on to tell them about a friend of mine who knows exactly what they are going through. My friend was a good man who was double-crossed by a buddy of his and wrongfully accused of a crime he didn't commit. When he was arrested in the dead of night, he immediately found himself abandoned by every one of the people he thought of as his friends and associates. Taken into custody, he was brutally punched and beaten by officers trying to extract a confession from him. As news spread about his arrest and the charges being brought against him, he was publicly denounced and disgraced. Awaiting trial, he was thrown into a rough prison cell without access to legal help. In a trial that was rigged from the beginning, he was summarily convicted of a capital offense and sentenced to death. More than I ever can, my friend understands what every prisoner experiences because he's been through the bad stuff, the worst that can happen in the name of justice. My friend's name is Jesus.

This experience of being an outsider going into prison comes to mind as I read Matthew's story of Jesus. In Matthew 1, he goes into great detail in portraying Jesus as being born within the lineage of a human family. His ancestry is traced back more than twenty generations, all the way to Abraham, and demonstrates not the pure pedigree of aristocracy, but a colorful lineage that includes heroes as well as rogues, forefathers of sterling character as well as those of sullied reputations, forebears with royal blood and others coming from common, even foreign, stock.

With all of this history as background, Jesus was born to a young couple in rather humble, if not difficult and even embarrassing circumstances. It was an inauspicious beginning for the man who would be known as the Savior of the world. The point Matthew is making is that Jesus' roots are historical, human roots in a real human family. He began His life just like us, helpless and dependent, and He is not an outsider who doesn't know what it is like to live as one of us.

There is great comfort in this because Jesus has experienced and knows the muck and mire of human living. He enters our world not with His eyes averted from our sordid failings and embarrassments, or with his heart closed to our inadequacies and impurity. Jesus understands what it is like for struggling men and women. The real Jesus is rooted in the continuing story of a man who knows life from the inside out.

According to Matthew, Jesus is one of us, and more. He is fully human and He is God, born in the humble soil of humankind. The starting point of faith is friendship with Jesus of Nazareth, because He understands and cares and sees us through everything we experience in being human—even in imprisonment and injustice. He is not only fully human in understanding and knows our problems and our anguish, but as God with us He is able to help us when we cannot even begin to help ourselves.

Through all this Matthew made it clear that Christ participates in our human generation and in our nature. Otherwise some might claim that he appeared in illusion and imagination only, rather than by becoming genuinely human. Think of what might have been said if none of this had been written? Severus of Antioch [1]

---

1 Cathedral Sermons, Homily 94, as quoted in *Ancient Christian Commentary on Scripture, New Testament* Vol. Ia, page 2 (2001, Inter Varsity Press, Downers Grove, IL; Ed. Thomas C. Oden).

CHAPTER 48

JESUS: HE'S THE MAN!

"He's the man; the leader we need for a time like this!" declared an American political pundit. "Obama has what it takes to reignite the spirit that made this country great." Yet neither Mr Obama nor the leader of any other country has what it takes to deliver all that is expected of a leader. In a world hungry for solutions, people desperately hinge their highest hopes on political leaders they look up to.

I can't imagine what it would be like to be the person in whom people put such great expectations and trust. On the one hand, it would be more than just a little frightening to consider the real possibility of failure or, at least, of disappointing the people who have placed their personal hope in me. On the other hand, it would be very gratifying to stand in the spotlight of the nation and the world, to be the man! There is a little something in every one of us craving for that kind of recognition, even if it be just a five-minute claim to fame.

Throughout history, leaders have emerged on to the world stage and have literally changed the world for better or worse. When John the Baptist arrived on the scene, he was certainly the man of the hour. Coming at a time when his people were subservient to an occupying foreign power, he seemed larger than life, like a prophet from the past who had come back to deliver them. If I had been in his sandals, I suppose it would have been difficult not to develop an inflated sense of significance in response to the popular adulation of the crowds coming out to hear and see; and their eager desire to be baptized in the Jordan River. As far as the people were concerned, John was clearly the man!

Yet John was very clear and quick to declare, "After me will come one more powerful than I, the thongs of whose sandals I am not worthy to stoop down and untie" (Mark 1:7). Unlike many of us, even in our small moments of attention and fame, John knew and publicly acknowledged that it wasn't about him.

Mark graphically makes this point as he begins telling the story of Jesus with a pithy declaration, "After John was put in prison" Jesus began proclaiming the good news of God. John, the baptizer and compelling personality, is summarily "dismissed" as the real story unfolds around Jesus. I sometimes wonder if John had not been put in prison, would he have been in competition with Jesus? Would the public have gravitated to John as the man and messenger, instead of to Jesus?

Yet Jesus arrives completely without John's help. For me this is a very cogent realization. Inevitably I struggle in preparing talks or articles and even conversations—how can I craft and deliver my message so that people will be convinced of Jesus? I feel so gratified when my words come out just right and when my delivery is articulate and persuasive; but when the words don't flow and I cannot seem to connect with people, I feel like a total failure.

Perhaps, at both my best and at my worst I tend to get in the way of Jesus. It should be clear that it is not about me or about how well I do or don't do. Jesus enters into human history and He alone radically transforms the world and the people of the world. It is not John the Baptist, Paul or Peter, or me or you who do that. As the story of salvation begins, so it continues. Jesus is the man!

> *"Any spiritual view which focuses attention on ourselves, and puts the human creature with its small ideas and adventures in the centre foreground, is dangerous till we recognize its absurdity ..."* [1]

---

1   *The Spiritual Life* by Evelyn Underhill (Morehouse Publishing, Harrisburg, PA; 1937).

CHAPTER 49

JESUS: SAVIOR OF THE WORLD

"Help! Help! I can't swim!" I was just twelve years old, quite tall for my age, and had just learned to swim during summer camp. Without even thinking I jumped into action, walking rather than swimming through shoulder-high water to where the kid was screaming and thrashing about. As he sank below the surface, I reached into the murky water of the lake and managed to grab hold of my fellow camper's arm. Lifting up and clutching him in a bear hug, I held his head above the water as I waddled awkwardly back toward shore where the lifeguards had just jumped from their stations, whistles blowing.

"Here he is," I stammered, my young body shaking with the rush of adrenalin. "He's OK now." With that, I deposited the wheezing camper in the shallows and waded back into the deeper water to continue swimming.

Word got around, and by evening everyone in camp was amazed at what I'd done. "You really saved him, didn't you?" they said in awe of my quicker-than-the-lifeguard response. Everyone held me for a hero except for the lifeguards and camp counselors, who were quick to deflate my sense of accomplishment, pointing out that I wasn't trained, had just barely learned to swim, and could easily have been dragged underwater and drowned by the pan-icked swimmer.

Their criticism hurt, but I knew they were right. Yet I also believed that if I hadn't acted when I did the life-guards would probably have been too late, or at best, the kid I saved would have had to be resuscitated. We all have a desire to help save the world, or at least to prevent some people from being hurt or from destroying themselves or each other and the environment we share. There are times we react with courage or compassion to save others. But there are also times when we cry out for help ourselves.

To many people, it seems that the world today is in trouble as deep as it has ever been. Consider the unend-ing litany of wars and conflicts, environmental disas-ters, famines, diseases, social ills, family violence, and economic ruin, not to mention the hatred and fear that afflicts millions upon millions of people. With more political leaders, church leaders, therapists, counselors, and financial advisors than the world has ever known, we would be hard pressed to say that we have come any closer to saving ourselves and the world we live in. We just can't seem to achieve a lasting solution for our per-sonal and global problems.

It has been the same in every age. There is a glimmer of hope for world peace and suddenly conflict breaks out anew. People search for physical, social, and spiritual ful-fillment through an ever-expanding array of options, only to discover that they are as unsatisfied and as restless as ever. Nations opt for increased security amid multiplying fears and uncertainty, only to find that security is not fail-safe. There seem to be no lasting solutions or prospect of salvation; no real exit from the darkness, depression, and disasters facing the world. At best all we can do is tune out reality or deny its hold on us. At the bitter end of it all, the only possibility is for a savior outside of us.

During an era that was as dark as ours, God radically entered His creation. It is as holy a mystery now as it was then, that Jesus became human to save humanity. The substance and the truth of the mystery is in the promise and the declaration that Jesus Christ is God incarnate, born into the midst of troubled humanity as Savior of the world by the tender mercy of God the Father.

This is the grand and cosmic declaration of Luke as he sets the stage for his account of the life of Jesus. Jesus the Christ, born of the Virgin Mary, has come to save the world, and salvation will be accomplished because He is God with us.

> *"The Holy Child to be born will be called the Son of God.*
> *... for the Mighty God has done great things...*
> *His name is Holy,*
> *His mercy sure from generation to generation.*
> *He has shown the might of His arm,*
> *He has routed the proud and all their schemes;*
> *He has brought down monarchs from their thrones,*
> *and raised on high the lowly.*
> *He has filled the hungry with good things,*
> *and sent the rich away empty.*
> *... as he promised to our forefathers;*

He has not forgotten to show mercy
... He has come and has redeemed his people.
He has raised up a horn of salvation for us...
salvation from our enemies
and from the hand of all who hate us –
to show mercy to our fathers ...
to rescue us from the hand of our enemies,
and to enable us to serve him without fear ...
to give his people knowledge of salvation,
through the forgiveness of their sins,
because of the tender mercy of our God,
by which the rising sun will come in us from heaven
to shine on those living in darkness
and in the shadow of death,
to guide our feet into the path of peace."

(Excerpts from Luke 1, *The Revised English Bible*)

CHAPTER 50

JESUS: THE LIGHT OF LIFE

"I know what you are talking about," declared the President, "because I was once a prisoner." Little did we know or expect that our visit with the President of Ecuador would be met with such understanding of the terrible things we had come to tell him about, the inhumane conditions in the prison, and the suffering being inflicted on prisoners as well as their families.

Invited to Ecuador some years ago by Dr Jorge Crespo Toral, human rights and labor lawyer, Chuck Colson and I had just visited Garcia Moreno prison and could hardly comprehend the tragedy of what we had seen and heard. It was unimaginable how anyone could survive imprisonment under such horrendous conditions: separated from their families, poor, and powerless. Prisoners told us stories of having been in prison for more than eight years and still waiting to appear before a judge. They felt completely forgotten, forsaken, and victimized. Together with Dr Crespo, we felt compelled to respond to the corruption, injustice, and hopelessness we had just seen.

With a measure of righteous audacity, Dr Crespo contacted the office of the President for an appointment. Miraculously, within an hour of leaving the prison, we found ourselves being ushered into the President's office. Immediately we began telling him what we had seen and heard of the prison conditions and the situation among the prisoners, and then we offered some possible solutions. The President, who had seemed receptive from the start, interrupted us with the story of his own experience as a prisoner.

"I was a political prisoner before democracy in our country, and I found myself not in any of the cells you saw during your visit today, but in an underground dungeon. There was no window, no light. It was utterly and completely dark. I was alone, afraid, becoming disoriented, and losing all sense of time. Suddenly there was an ominous noise as the big steel door creaked open. In mortal fear, I crouched in the damp corner of my dungeon, knowing that the soldiers had come to get me and that I would never see my family again. While I was still trembling, the door creaked slowly on its steel hinges as the person who had come into my cell left as inexplicably as he had come. All of a sudden there was an explosion of light! I was terrified until I realized that it was just a simple light bulb. The darkness was gone and I came to learn that a fellow prisoner had risked his life to bring me light. From that moment on I knew I would live, because I had light!"

There was a short pause and then the President continued. "If I understand what you are telling me, this is what you propose to do, to bring light into the prison."

We were astounded and could not have agreed more. We continued discussing practical things that could be done to alleviate prisoners' suffering, to reform the criminal justice system, and to implement meaningful programs for the prison inmates. It wasn't long before the President pronounced, "The prisons of this country are open for you to do as you have said."

There is no doubt that every one of the possibilities we outlined that day would have injected a measure of hope into the dreadful darkness of imprisonment. While we were, in fact, able to implement several initiatives and make some progress, corruption within the system, political instability, and the self-interest of government officials continued to undermine our best efforts.

John's story about the coming of Jesus is likewise a gripping story of light breaking into darkness. "In him was life" declares John, "and that life was the light of all people. The light shines in the darkness, and the darkness has not understood it" (John 1:4-5). However, the story John tells has a very different ending than the story of our best attempts to prevail against the darkness of inhumanity, injustice, and corruption in the prison system.

John exults in the story of real and lasting hope breaking into the darkness of human history through Jesus, "For God so loved the world that he gave his one and only Son, that whoever believes in him shall not perish but have eternal life. For God did not send his Son into the world to condemn the world, but to save the world through him ... this is the verdict: Light has come into the world ...." (John 3:16-17, 19). John goes on to tell how Jesus proclaims and demonstrates this new reality. "I am the light of the world," says Jesus. "Whoever follows me will never walk in darkness, but will have the light of life" (John 8:12).

The light of Jesus dispels the darkness, infusing human-kind with hope and light. This story of Jesus isn't finished yet, for there are still people and powers that prefer dark-ness to light, evil to goodness. And it is a story that con-tinues to be played out in our hearts and relationships as the radical story of light penetrating the darkness of human failure and futility.

> *Our choice is this. It is to choose to believe that the truth of our story is contained in Jesus' story, which is a love story. Jesus' story is the truth about who we are and who the God is who Jesus says loves us. It is the truth about where we are going and how we are going to get there, if we get there at all, and what we are going to find if we finally do. Only for once let us not betray the richness and depth and mystery of that truth by trying to explain it.* [1]

---

1 Frederick Buechner (*Secrets in the Dark: A Life in Sermons:* Harper Collins, New York, 2006).

Chapter 51

JESUS: THE SHAPE OF GOD

A quotation often attributed to Blaise Pascal states that, "There is a God shaped vacuum in the heart of every man which cannot be filled by any created thing, but only by God, the Creator." [1]

A provocative study suggests that there is a relationship between our concept of God and our attitudes to economics, justice, social morality, politics, love, and life in general. [2] The shape of God in our lives affects our worldview.

"Your God is too small!" wrote J.B. Phillips [3] in a book that challenged my concept of God many years ago. Among the "small" notions of God that he exposed were those of the "resident policeman," the God of burly legalism and summary judgment; the "grand old man" of ancient his-

---

1 There is no evidence that Pascal, the French mathematician, actually wrote these words. Most likely this statement has been extracted from a passage in *Pensées* (#425) "What else does this craving, and this helplessness, proclaim but that there was once in man a true happiness, of which all that now remains is the empty print and trace? This he tries in vain to fill with everything around him, seeking in things that are not there the help he cannot find in those that are, though none can help, since this infinite abyss can be filled only with an infinite and immutable object; in other words by God himself."

2 *America's Four Gods*, Paul Froese and Christopher Bader (Oxford University Press, 2010).

3 *Your God is Too Small*, J.B. Phillips (Macmillan Press, London, 1961).

tory, the God who is tired and removed from the clamor of modern life; "absolute perfection," the God whose unqualified demands are unrealistic and impossible for humanity to attain; "managing director," the God who is concerned with the complex issues of the universe but not involved or interested in the petty little details of human life and death.

Phillips' book had a powerful impact on me, and little by little I began to realize that I had replaced the fearful "God as policeman" of my youth with an equally erroneous notion of God as "managing director," who cannot be counted on, or called upon, to be concerned or involved with the adventures and mishaps of my life. Both of these concepts or shapes of God found expression through my social attitudes and behavior. The contemporary study, though very different from J.B. Phillips' book,[4] similarly describes four different notions of God and how these affect individual perceptions and relationships to the world. Not surprisingly, the four shapes of God are directly correlated with social and political attitudes.

The shape of God as authoritative focuses on moral, social, and political expectations. This view is often reflected in demands for conformity and the explicit or implicit exclusion of those groups who don't conform to our core beliefs and moral values. Rooted in our authoritative concept of God, we tend to marginalize and reject such people on the basis of inclusion or exclusion from God's favor. They are either good or evil, with us or against us.

---

4   ibid.

During frequent travels in Asia and the Middle East, I have encountered the hostility of social and political damage caused by people who denounce others on the basis of religious differences.

A contrasting shape to the authoritative God is the benevolent God who embraces the world and who loves and cares for all people. This notion of God is reflected in open engagement with people in need, regardless of their creed or culture. This view of God idealizes and seeks to express God's unconditional love by serving the poor, caring for prisoners, embracing immigrants and refugees, and defending the exploited.

Inevitably, the most powerful witness I have seen among prisoners has far more to do with love and acceptance than with moralizing and judgment. I find that broken people are attracted more to someone who loves them than to someone who preaches at them. Often in dealing with unsavory characters I need to remind myself that the good news of the gospel is Jesus, the one sent by God, who so greatly loved the world that He did not come to condemn the world and its people but to save (John 3:16-17).

A third shape of God is the critical God who keeps a precise record of good and evil in the world, but who will ultimately act only by delivering justice in the world to come. This notion of God reflects in a kind of detachment or resignation in the face of human suffering and injustice. Healing and judgment are both deferred to the coming of God's Kingdom, the life hereafter when all good will be rewarded and all evil punished. The condition of the world and the social problems around us are not our problems, not our responsibility. There is no need to take responsibility in responding to other people's problems, no need to confront evil and injustice, no need to be politically active. It is enough to pray and to believe, hoping for the coming of God's Kingdom when He will set things right.

The fourth shape of God is that of the distant God who created the world and set things in motion, but who is no longer involved with the world and its people. It is difficult, if not impossible, to really know this God personally for He is remote. Although the world was formed by Him, what happens now is simply the continuing struggle between human advancement and inhumanity, between good and bad. Belief in the existence of God is one thing, but in the real world we are left to be masters of our own destiny and captains of our own fate.

In thinking about these four views, or shapes, of God I can't help but wonder what the God-shaped vacuum in our lives looks like? Today, tomorrow, and the next day our concept of God will inevitably be expressed through our attitudes, relationships, work, and politics.

If we think of God as being strict and judgmental, then we can easily demand tough prison conditions and the punishment of prisoners until "their debt to society is paid." On the other hand, if we understand God as truly compassionate and loving, caring for sinners and suffering with those who suffer, we have reason to join Him in works of love and mercy by caring for the needy and embracing offenders with the possibility of forgiveness and freedom. And if we see God as a cosmic record-keeper who will ultimately reward all good, punish all evil, and rectify all wrongs, then we will tend to insulate ourselves from the issues of the world by attending to our own affairs and letting God take care of the rest. If we see God as an impersonal supreme being who has abdicated everything to human responsibility, then our lives will tend to lean toward improving the quality of our lives and that of others here and now without any spiritual connection or meaning.

The radically good news of Jesus is that He is the shape of God perfectly expressed in the rough and tumble of human life. When humanity had lost sight of its connection with God, when human beings had become disappointed by the God they could not hear or see; when most people had given up all hope in a God whose promises seemed remote, then God became incarnate in Jesus of Nazareth to demonstrate the truth of how much He really loves humankind.

"No one is ever really at ease in facing what we call 'life' and 'death' without a religious faith. The trouble with many people today is that they have not found a God big enough for modern needs. While their experience of life has grown in a score of directions, and their mental horizons have been expanded to the point of bewilderment by world events and by scientific discoveries, their ideas of God have remained largely static. It is obviously impossible for an adult to worship the conception of God that exists in the mind of a child ... unless he is prepared to deny his own experience of life. If, by a great effort of will, he does do this he will

always be secretly afraid lest some new truth may expose the juvenility of his faith. And it will always be by such an effort that he either worships or serves a God who is really too small to command his adult loyalty and co-operation." [5]

5   J.B. Phillips op.cit (from the Introduction).

CHAPTER 52

JESUS: OUR LIVING HOPE

' Just as man cannot live without dreams, he cannot live without hope. If dreams reflect the past, hope summons the future. Does this mean that our future can be built on a rejection of the past? Surely such a choice is not necessary. The two are incompatible. The opposite of the past is not the future, but the absence of future ...' [1]

I was with suffering prisoners in a miserable prison in Africa as rumors of clemency circulated like wildfire and prisoners' hopes were ignited by a glimmer of possible freedom. Several months later those hopes were realized for more than 1,500 prisoners who were among those named in a presidential order for clemency.[2] But for thousands of others throughout the country it was yet another bitter disappointment, their hopes squelched by brutal reality.

"Hope," declared Friedrich Nietzsche, the German philosopher who proclaimed 'the death of God,' "is the

---

1   Elie Wiesel. Nobel Lecture, December 11, 1986 http://www.english.illinois.edu/maps/holocaust/wiesel.htm

2   The order was cited as the Clemency Order Number 1 of 2009, published in the Government Gazette of Zimbabwe of 21 August 2009.

worst of all evils, because it prolongs man's torments." [3]
Like so many other prisoners around the world who hope
in vain for amnesty and pardon, those who remained
imprisoned while others received amnesty experienced
the torment of hope that proves to be false. Yet many
whose hopes for clemency were realized entered a future
that was just as painful as the past by which they were
defined—thieves, addicts, ex-convicts! Their hope for a
future of freedom from the miserable present and the
past was likewise shattered. Many whose families had
abandoned them, and who could find no place to live
or work, found themselves back where they had come
from, imprisoned again. Hope for a brighter future did
not sustain them.

Most of us have also placed hope in people, promises, and particular circumstances only to experience
those hopes disintegrating into hurtful disappointments.
Just when we count on them, most promises are broken,
finances don't stretch far enough, plans fall apart, and the
breakthrough we anticipated just doesn't happen. We find
ourselves back where we were, or even worse.

"Faint Hope" is a provision in the Criminal Code of
Canada that provides life-sentenced prisoners with the
opportunity to apply for early parole after serving fifteen
years of their sentence. The idea behind "faint hope" is
to extend a small measure of hope to people who would
otherwise have no hope or possibility of release from

---

3 Friedrich Nietzsche (*"Human: All-Too-Human"*—Nietzsche's collection of
almost 1,400 aphorisms published by the University of Nebraska Press, 1986.

prison.[4] In reality, "faint hope" lives up to its name, for it offers no real hope and no guarantee of parole at all, merely the opportunity to apply for parole that is often denied. Prisoners who apply for parole under this provision inevitably find themselves grasping at straws that offer no assurance that their hope for freedom will be realized.

Like prisoners, many people live in a cyclical, cynical world of hope and disappointment where today's hope becomes tomorrow's disappointment. What masquerades through our lives as hope is often nothing more than the projected desires of others, our own wishful thinking, or the convergence of both. We cannot live without hope and yet our hopes are often faint and false. Many become prisoners in their own thinking, afraid of getting their hopes up for fear of being disappointed.

"Hope is a dangerous thing," said actor Morgan Freeman's character in *The Shawshank Redemption*[5] as a fellow prisoner talked about his hope for freedom. For Freeman's character, the very idea of hope was painfully intolerable because he had completely given up on freedom; he couldn't see beyond the prison bars and was resigned to the fact that his life would end in prison. In

---

4 The faint-hope clause, or judicial review, section 745.6 of the Canadian Criminal Code, states that prisoners serving the maximum sentence of life in prison without the possibility of parole for 25 years may apply for early parole after serving 15 years. The clause was added to the Criminal Code after Parliament abolished the death penalty in 1976 and replaced it with mandatory life terms of imprisonment for first-degree and second-degree murder.

5 The 1994 motion picture *The Shawshank Redemption*.

total contrast to his experience, "Prisoners of Hope" [6] is how Dayna Curry and Heather Mercer described their ordeal of capture and imprisonment by the Taliban in Afghanistan. Sustained by their faith and hope in God as they faced their ordeal, they knew that their futures were not in the hands of the Taliban, but in the hands of the Lord. Unlike Morgan Freeman's character, they were not prisoners of fear, futility, and fate, but prisoners of hope.

"Prisoners of hope," is what the prophet Zechariah (9:12) calls the faithful, hopeful remnant of believers in God living among a people in captivity, a remnant clinging to God's promise of deliverance and restoration despite all evidence to the contrary. They were not enslaved by false or faint hope but were liberated by hope, refusing to be resigned to captivity as their inevitable fate.

Each year during Advent, I think anew about the radical nature of hope in Jesus. It is an audacious and dangerous hope, rising above every false and faint hope. It is the hope that supersedes all hope for it centers on God, who engaged with humanity through Jesus in order to bring about ultimate freedom. It is no ordinary hope, but a radical hope. It is hope in Jesus the Liberator, Jesus the Prince of Peace, Jesus, the Son of God Almighty, who has already come and who will come again to redeem and restore.

---

6   Dayna Curry and Heather Mercer; *Prisoners of Hope* (Waterbrook Press, Colorado Springs, USA; 2003).

... we wait for the blessed hope—
the glorious appearing of our great God and Savior,
*   Jesus Christ,*
who gave himself for us to redeem us from all
*   wickedness*
and to purify for himself a people that are his very own,
eager to do what is good. (Titus 2:13-14)

CHAPTER 53

PAUSE AT THE THRESHOLD

"Just one month, three weeks, fourteen hours and, let's see ... about forty-five minutes to go." This was not an early countdown to the New Year, but a typical response from a prisoner anticipating the day and minute of his release. That is the threshold of hope for which many prisoners exist, when life resumes and when freedom and happiness will be theirs again. At least that is the myth among people in captivity who take the measure of their lives in time served and time remaining to be served.

For many of us, the end of one year and the beginning of a new year represents a similar kind of threshold, with fresh beginnings and new possibilities. This is particularly true as we turn the page on the difficulties of the past year to the new page of the coming year. The opportunity for a new beginning and the promise of things to come is anticipated along with all the possibilities that the threshold of a new year represents. Release from the stifling confines of the past year into the fresh beginning of a new year!

I find the threshold of a new year both daunting and exhilarating. For me it represents more than just the desire for new physical, mental, social, and spiritual possibilities, but the opportunity to renew and consolidate my intentions for living a better life. As I cross the threshold from the previous year, I desire to be more productive and more disciplined than last year. So I pause at the threshold to take stock of my life.

There is a nagging problem for, like you, I have been on thresholds like this before. Along with my prisoner friends, I have ended up being imprisoned in the same problems and disappointments all over again. I suppose this is the perennial reality of being human, for even as times change we remain the same people we have always been, with all of our hopes and all of our history.

Mark Twain observed that it is an optimist "who travels on nothing from nowhere to happiness." Many of us have approached the threshold of a new year as optimists and, upon stepping across that threshold, find ourselves enmeshed with the same problems, personalities, and passions that we ended the previous year. The freedom and happiness we anticipated is inevitably obscured by the fact that we are not new. In fact, we travel from somewhere with something and discover that the things we have accumulated along the way cross over the threshold with us.

So crossing the threshold of a new year gives me pause to reflect on my journey and all of the things I am bringing with me. I carry valuable nuggets of faith and friendship, but also undesirable things like memories of nagging failure, bitter disappointments, and festering resentments. Do I really need to take these with me into the new year, or can I really leave them behind? Will past disappointments ever help and strengthen me in my journey, or memories of personal insult and injury, or guilt of failures past, or worry over unknown futures, or the aching pain of loss?

As I pause at the threshold of a new year, I look to the Lord to enable me to leave behind all those things that will distract and hinder me in my journey. I desire to enter into the beginning of another year growing in companionship with Jesus—caring about the things He cares about, and loving others as radically as He loves them.

Prayer for the new year [1]

O God of new beginnings and wonderful surprises,
   thank you for the gift of a new year.
May it be a time of grace for me.
      a time to grow in faith and love,
      a time to renew my commitment to following your
         Son, Jesus.
May it be a year of blessing for me,
      a time to cherish my family and friends,
      a time to renew my efforts at work,
      a time to embrace my faith more fully.
Walk with me, please, in every day and every hour of
      this new year,
      that the light of Christ might shine through me,
      in spite of my weaknesses and failings.
Above all, may I remember this year that I am a pilgrim
      on the sacred path to You.
      Amen

---

1   Quoted from the website St. Agnes Cathedral (January 1, 2008) www. stagnescathedral.org/Parish/prayers/newyear.htm